NIKON D7200

THE EXPANDED GUIDE

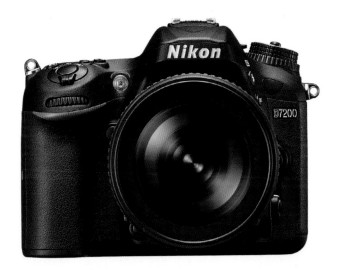

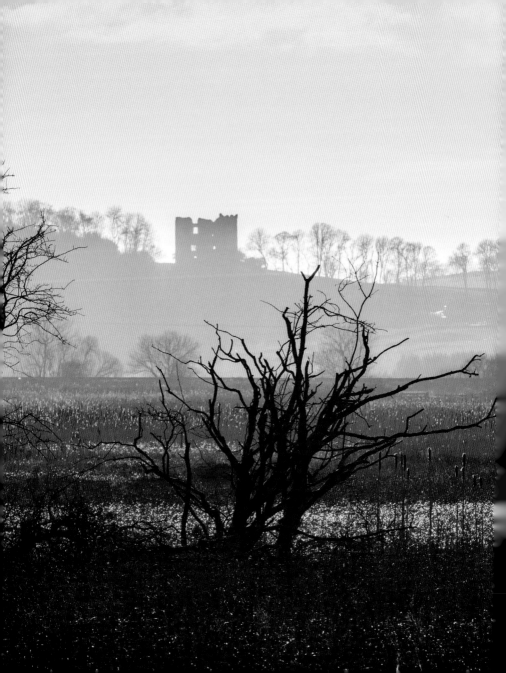

NIKON D7200

THE EXPANDED GUIDE

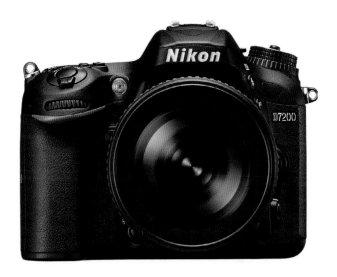

Jon Sparks

AMMONITE
PRESS

First published 2015 by
Ammonite Press
an imprint of AE Publications Ltd
166 High Street, Lewes, East Sussex, BN7 1XU, UK

Text © AE Publications Ltd, 2015
Images © Jon Sparks 2015 (unless otherwise specified)
Copyright © in the Work AE Publications Ltd, 2015

ISBN 978-1-78145-229-5

British Library Cataloging in Publication Data: A catalog
record of this book is available from the British Library.

Editor: Rob Yarham
Series Editor: Richard Wiles
Design: Richard Dewing Associates

Typefaces: Giacomo
Color reproduction by GMC Reprographics
Printed in China

« PAGE 2
DARK TOWER
The D7200 can deliver excellent
image quality even under difficult
conditions, and this book will help
you make the most of it.
*170mm, 1/640 sec., f/10,
ISO 100.*

» CONTENTS

1 OVERVIEW

The D7200 is now being hailed as the flagship model in Nikon's range of DX-format cameras. It combines an impressive feature set and rugged build while remaining relatively compact and lightweight. Versatile and durable, it is ideal for enthusiasts and semi-professional photographers. Indeed, it has all the features and functions to meet the needs of many full-time professional photographers.

» EVOLUTION OF THE NIKON D7200

Nikon has long been admired for blending innovation and continuity. For example, when the main manufacturers introduced their first viable autofocus 35mm cameras in the 1980s, most jettisoned their existing lens mounts, but Nikon stayed true to its established F-mount system. It's still possible to use many classic Nikon lenses with the latest digital cameras like the D7200, although some camera functions may be lost. For this and other reasons, "evolution" is an appropriate word to describe the development of Nikon's digital cameras.

Nikon's first real digital SLRs (DSLRs) were the E2 and E2s, in 1995. Sporting a then-impressive 1.3-megapixel sensor, the body design was based on the F-801 35mm SLR.

However, the true line of descent of the D7200 begins in 1999, with the 2.7-megapixel D1. Its sensor adopted the DX format (see page 10), which was a constant in every Nikon DSLR until the introduction of the "full-frame" (FX-format) D3 in 2007.

SHIP SHAPE »
The Nikon D7200, together with the wide range of Nikon system lenses and accessories, provides you with lots of flexibility for exploring and experimenting with your photography.
18mm, 1/80 sec., f/11, ISO 100.

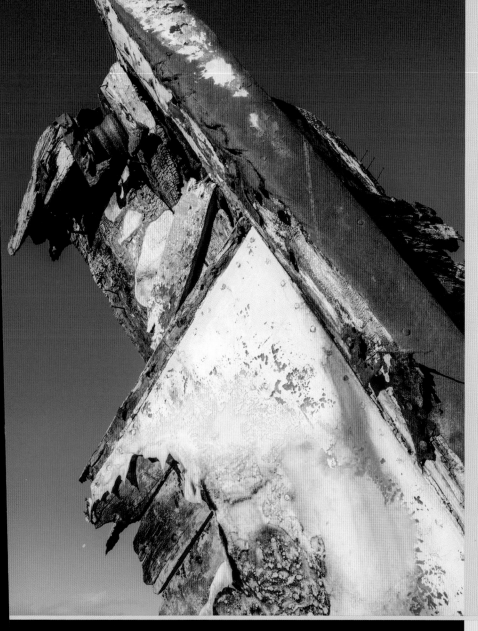

1 › Evolution of the Nikon D7200

Nikon continued to develop both its FX and DX ranges; a notable debutant was the D7000 in 2010. This 16-megapixel camera was the first DX-format Nikon DSLR to deliver Full HD movie recording and proved a hit with stills photographers too, both amateur and professional.

Like the rest of the Japanese camera industry, Nikon suffered severe disruption following the earthquake and tsunami of March 2011. While the bulk of its manufacturing now takes place outside Japan (notably in Malaysia), some crucial components are still made in Japan, and research and development is centered there. However, the company showed every sign of making up for lost time in 2012. The FX-format launches (D800 and D600) may have been the most talked about, but the DX-format D3200 and D5200 were more relevant to a wider range of users.

Early in 2013, the D7100 completed a comprehensive refresh of the DX range, with all models now mustering 24 million pixels. Of course, opinions vary on the wisdom of ever-increasing pixel counts, but so far, Nikon continues to extract excellent all-round image quality.

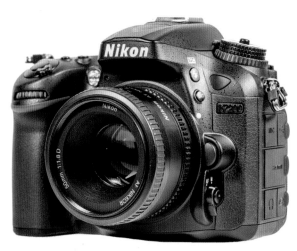

Nikon D7200

Nikon D1 (1999)

With 2.7 million pixels, the D1's specification now seems feeble, yet it is arguably the most significant digital camera launch of all time, making digital truly practical and cost-effective.

Nikon D90 (2008)

The D90 had many new features, but one of these grabbed all the headlines as it became the first DSLR capable of shooting video.

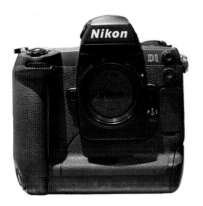

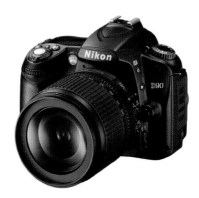

Nikon D300s (2009)

Nikon's line of fully professional DX cameras, which began with the D1, seems to have ended with the exceptionally rugged D300s, as full-frame (FX) DSLRs become more widespread.

Nikon D7100 (2013)

On the surface a modest upgrade to the D7000, the D7100 had some significant changes under the skin, notably becoming the first mainstream Nikon DSLR to dispense with an "anti-aliasing" filter in front of its sensor.

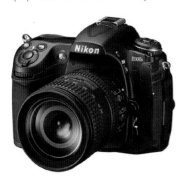

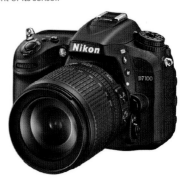

1

› About the Nikon D7200

In most respects, the D7200 is a consolidation of the successful D7100, but there are some significant changes. The pixel count remains the same (give or take a fraction) but the sensor is a different model, expected to deliver better dynamic range.

Many pundits predict that the D300s (still available but looking rather long in the tooth) will be the last DX-format DSLR officially classified as a professional camera. Nikon neither confirm nor deny this, but emphasis has clearly shifted to the FX lineup. However, the D7200 is solidly built and weather-sealed, if not quite as bombproof as the D300s.

One very notable advance over the D7100 is a much improved buffer; this makes it possible to capture longer continuous bursts of images even when shooting RAW. Battery life has also been improved.

In addition, the D7200 gains onboard Wi-Fi, allowing the camera to be triggered from a smartphone or tablet. Both the image processor and the autofocus module are new versions. Among other benefits, this improves the camera's ability to focus in low light.

Like all Nikon DSLRs, the D7200 is part of a vast system of lenses, accessories, and software. This Expanded Guide to the Nikon D7200 will guide you through all aspects of the camera's operation, and its relation to the system as a whole.

› Nikon DX-format sensors

DX-format sensors, measuring approximately 23.5 x 15.6mm (with slight variations), featured in every Nikon DSLR from the D1 onward, until the arrival of "full-frame" FX-format cameras (e.g. D4, D800, D600). However, the number of pixels on the sensor has risen from 2.7 million on the D1 to around 24 million across the current DX range. Early models used CCD sensors but today CMOS (Complementary Metal Oxide Semiconductor) sensors are used across Nikon's DSLR range.

The DX format dictates a 1.5x magnification factor, relative to the same lenses used on 35mm and FX cameras. The D7200's CMOS sensor measures 23.5 x 15.6 mm, making it fractionally smaller than some other models. Its 24 million pixels deliver images at a native size of 6000 x 4000 pixels, making them suitable for demanding large prints and book and magazine reproduction.

Starting with the D7100, Nikon has dispensed with an "anti-aliasing" filter in front of the sensor in new models. The effect of this should be to make images even sharper, and results do seem to bear this out—but the difference will only show up with good lenses and good technique.

FOCUSING ON THE DETAILS »
Twenty four million pixels is more than enough to deliver crisp detail for almost any purpose.
95mm, 1/500 sec., f/11, ISO 200.

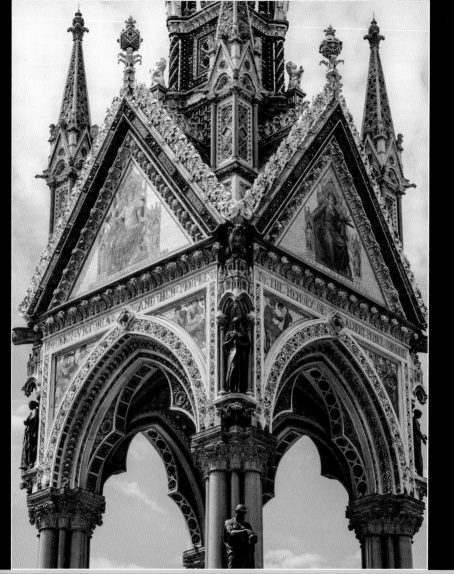

1 » MAIN FEATURES OF THE NIKON D7200

Sensor

24 effective megapixel DX-format RGB CMOS sensor measuring 23.5 x 15.6mm and producing maximum image size of 6000 x 4000 pixels; 1.3x crop option; self-cleaning function. No optical low-pass (anti-aliasing) filter.

Image processor

EXPEED 4 image processing system featuring 14-bit analog-to-digital (A/D) conversion with 16-bit image processing.

Focus

Nikon Multi-CAM 3500DX II autofocus module featuring 51 autofocus points. Three focus modes: (S) Single-servo AF; (C) Continuous-servo AF; and (M) Manual focus. Three AF-area modes: Single-area AF; Dynamic-area AF with option of 3D tracking; and Auto-area AF. Rapid focus point selection and focus lock.

Exposure

Three metering modes: matrix metering; center-weighted metering; spot metering. 3D Color Matrix Metering II uses a 2016-segment color sensor to analyze data on brightness, color, contrast, and subject distance from all areas of the frame. With non-G/D/E-Type lenses, Standard Color Matrix Metering II is employed. Two fully auto modes: auto; auto (flash off). Four user-controlled modes: (P) Programmed auto with flexible program; (A) Aperture-priority auto; (S) Shutter-priority auto; (M) Manual. 16 Scene modes: portrait; landscape; child; sports; close-up; night portrait; night landscape; party/indoor; beach/snow; sunset; dusk/dawn; pet portrait; candlelight; blossom; autumn colors; food. Two user-settings modes. Seven Effects modes. ISO range between 100 and 25,600, plus additional mono-only settings of 51,200 and 102,400. Exposure compensation between −5 Ev and +5 Ev; exposure lock and exposure bracketing facility.

Shutter

Shutter speeds from 1/8000 sec. to 30 sec., plus Bulb. Maximum frame advance 6fps (7fps with 1.3x crop). Quiet mode, self-timer, remote control, and mirror-up modes.

Viewfinder and Live View

Bright viewfinder with 100% coverage and 0.94x magnification; diopter adjustment between −2 and +1 m^{-1}. Live View available on rear LCD monitor.

Movie mode

Continuous feed in Live View mode allows movie capture in .MOV format (H.264/MPEG-4 compression) with image size (pixels) of: 1280 x 720, 1920 x 1080. Frame rates 60/50/30/25/24fps at large size; 60/50fps at small size.

Buffer

Buffer capacity allows up to 100 JPEG frames to be captured in a continuous burst at 6fps, approximately 16 NEF (RAW) files.

Built-in flash

Pop-up flash with Guide Number of 12 (m) or 39 (ft) at ISO 100 supports i-TTL balanced fill-flash for DSLR (when matrix or center-weighted metering is selected) and Standard i-TTL flash for DSLR (when spot metering is selected). Five flash sync modes: Front-curtain sync; Red-eye reduction; Slow sync; Red-eye reduction with slow sync; Rear-curtain sync. Flash compensation to +/– 3 Ev; FV lock.

LCD monitor

High-definition 3.2-inch, 1,229,000-pixel (VGA) TFT LCD display with 100% frame coverage.

Custom functions

51 parameters and elements of the camera's operations can be customized through the Custom setting menu.

File formats

The D7200 supports NEF (RAW) (14-bit and 12-bit) and JPEG (Fine/Normal/Basic) file formats.

Storage

Dual Secure Digital (SD) card slots; accepts SDHC and SDXC cards. Compatible with more than 60 current and many non-current Nikkor lenses (functionality varies with older lenses); SB-series flashguns; Multi-Power Battery Pack MB-D15; GP-1 GPS unit; Stereo Microphone ME-1; and many other Nikon system accessories.

Software

Supplied with Nikon View NX-i (incorporates Nikon Transfer 2); compatible with Nikon Capture NX-D and many third-party imaging applications.

1 » FULL FEATURES AND CAMERA LAYOUT

FRONT OF CAMERA

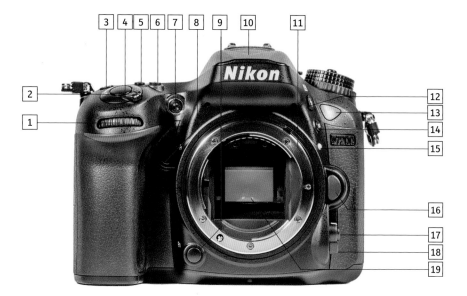

1	Sub-command dial	11	Lens mount
2	Shutter-release button	12	Flash button
3	Exposure compensation button	13	Front infrared receiver
4	Power switch	14	Bracketing button
5	Movie-record button	15	Lens mounting index mark
6	Metering/format button	16	Lens release button
7	AF-assist illuminator/Self-timer/Red-eye reduction lamp	17	AF mode button
8	Preview (Pv) button	18	Focus mode selector
9	Function (Fn) button	19	Mirror
10	Built-in flash		

BACK OF CAMERA

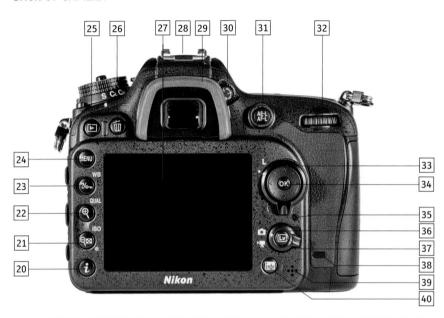

20	i button	
21	Zoom out/Thumbnail/ISO button	
22	Zoom in/Qual button	
23	Protect/help/white balance button	
24	MENU button	
25	Playback button	
26	Delete button	
27	LCD monitor screen	
28	Accessory hotshoe	
29	Viewfinder eyepiece	
30	Diopter adjustment dial	

31	AE-L/AF-L button
32	Main command dial
33	Multi-selector
34	OK button
35	Memory card access lamp
36	Live View mode selector
37	Live View button
38	Infrared receiver (rear)
39	Speaker
40	Info button

1 » FULL FEATURES AND CAMERA LAYOUT

TOP OF CAMERA

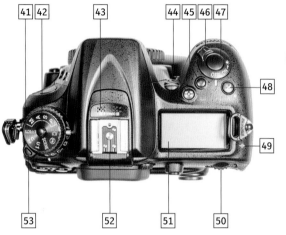

LEFT SIDE

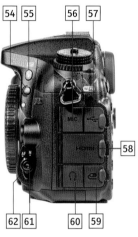

41 Mode dial	**50** Main command dial	**54** BKT button	
42 Mode dial lock release button	**51** LCD control panel	**55** Flash button	
43 Stereo microphones	**52** Accessory hotshoe	**56** External microphone	
44 Metering/format button	**53** Release mode dial lock release button	**57** USB connector	
45 Movie-record button		**58** HDMI connector cover	
46 Power switch		**59** Accessory terminal connector	
47 Shutter-release button		**60** Headphone jack	
48 Exposure compensation button		**61** AF mode button	
49 Focal plane mark		**62** Focus mode selector	

BOTTOM OF CAMERA

RIGHT SIDE

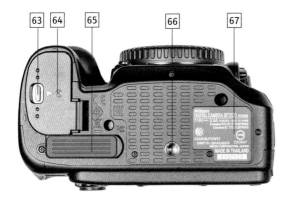

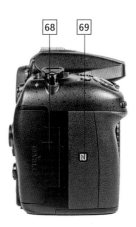

63	Battery compartment release lock
64	Battery compartment
65	External battery pack contact cover
66	Tripod socket (¼in.)
67	Camera serial number

| 68 | Memory card slot cover |
| 69 | NFC (Near Field Communication) |

1 » LCD CONTROL PANEL

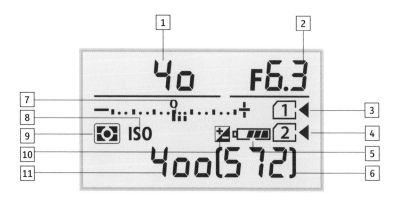

1	Shutter speed
2	Aperture
3	Memory card indicator (Slot 1)
4	Memory card indicator (Slot 2)
5	Battery indicator
6	Number of exposures remaining
7	Analog exposure display
8	ISO sensitivity indicator/Auto sensitivity indicator
9	Metering
10	Exposure compensation indicator
11	ISO sensitivity

» VIEWFINDER DISPLAY

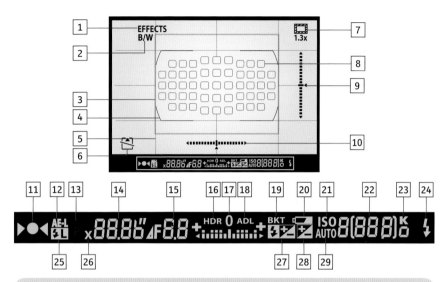

1	Effects mode indicator	12	AE lock indicator
2	Monochrome indicator	13	Flexible program indicator
3	1.3x DX crop outline	14	Shutter speed
4	AF area brackets	15	Aperture
5	Framing grid	16	HDR indicator
6	No memory card warning	17	Analog exposure display
7	1.3x DX crop indicator	18	ADL (Active D-Lighting) indicator
8	Focus points	19	Bracketing indicator
9	Roll indicator (portrait orientation)	20	Low battery warning
10	Roll indicator (landscape orientation)	21	ISO sensitivity indicator
11	Focus indicator	22	Number of exposures remaining/number of

1. Effects mode indicator
2. Monochrome indicator
3. 1.3x DX crop outline
4. AF area brackets
5. Framing grid
6. No memory card warning
7. 1.3x DX crop indicator
8. Focus points
9. Roll indicator (portrait orientation)
10. Roll indicator (landscape orientation)
11. Focus indicator
12. AE lock indicator
13. Flexible program indicator
14. Shutter speed
15. Aperture
16. HDR indicator
17. Analog exposure display
18. ADL (Active D-Lighting) indicator
19. Bracketing indicator
20. Low battery warning
21. ISO sensitivity indicator
22. Number of exposures remaining/number of exposures remaining in buffer/preset manual white balance recording indicator
23. "K" (when over 1000 exposures remain)
24. Flash-ready indicator
25. FV lock indicator
26. Flash sync indicator
27. Flash compensation indicator
28. Exposure compensation indicator
29. Auto ISO sensitivity indicator

2 FUNCTIONS

The Nikon D7200 has 19 separate buttons, half a dozen dials and switches, and hundreds of items in its menus. If this plethora of controls seems overwhelming, it's important to realize that you don't have to master them all at once. The D7200 can be used as simply as any "point-and-shoot" camera, but will still deliver far superior image quality. It arrives set to its simplest operating mode ⒶUTO and you can revert at any time by returning the mode dial to this position.

You can also quickly reset almost all other camera settings to the initial default by holding down the 🄴 and 🔍 buttons (marked with green dots) for at least 2 seconds; this is known as a two-button reset.

However, all those buttons and dials are a sign that the camera offers great versatility and imaging power. Leaving it at default settings misses out on much of this, but you don't need to dive in at the deep end either. The key is understanding which modes and which settings are suited to your photography. A great

starting point is by exploring Scene modes (pages 40–45).

This chapter will cover the location and use of the main controls and explore the main shooting modes and other functions. The following chapter delves into the menus.

OUT AND ABOUT »

When you unpack a new camera, it's tempting to start shooting right away—and taking pictures is the best way to learn. However, it still makes sense to peruse this book first, to ensure you don't miss out on new features and functions. *50mm, 1/125 sec., f/10, ISO 200.*

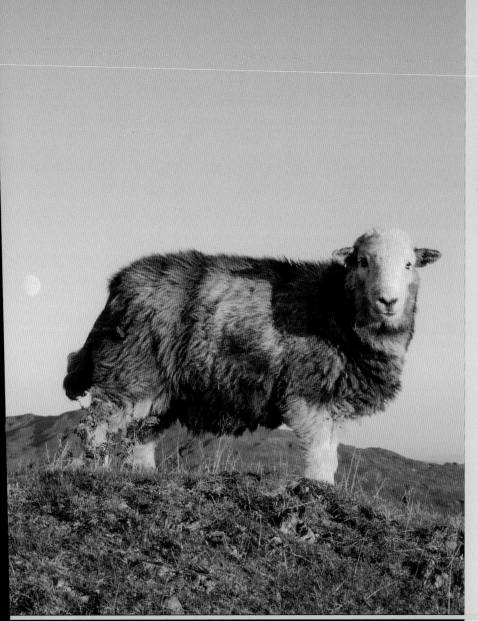

2 » CAMERA PREPARATION

Some operations, like charging the battery and inserting a memory card, are essential before you can use the camera. When first switched on, the camera will also prompt you to set language time, date, and time zone: see under **Setup menu**, page 130.

› Inserting the battery

The supplied EN-EL15 li-ion rechargeable battery should be fully charged before first use. Locate the battery compartment in the base of the camera. Release the latch to open the compartment. Insert the battery, contacts first, with the flat face towards the lens. Nudge the gold-colored latch aside with the battery, then slide the battery gently in until the latch clicks home. Close the compartment cover, ensuring it locks. To remove the battery, switch off the camera, and open the cover as above. Push the gold latch to release the battery, then slide it out of the compartment.

› Charging the battery

Using the supplied MH-25 charger, plugged into the mains, a full recharge takes around 2½ hours.

Align the battery, terminals first, with the slot on the charger; it will only fit the slot when correctly orientated. Slide the battery into the slot until it snaps home. The Charge lamp blinks during charging, and shines steadily when charging is complete.

INSERTING THE BATTERY ⌄

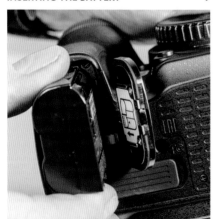

CHARGING THE BATTERY ⌄

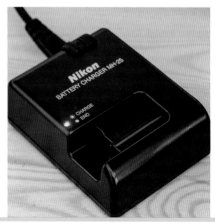

› Battery life

Various factors influence battery life. The LCD screen, built-in flash, and lens autofocus motors all draw power from the battery. Long meter-off delays reduce battery life. Extensive Live View and movie shooting are particularly draining. Extreme cold can also shorten battery life.

Under stringent (CIPA) test conditions, around 1110 shots can be taken between recharges. You can easily beat this figure if you shoot using the viewfinder, focus manually, and minimize screen use (e.g. changing settings, reviewing shots).

The control panel gives an approximate indication of remaining charge. This icon blinks when the battery is exhausted. A warning icon appears in the viewfinder when it is approaching exhaustion. **Battery Info** (Setup menu) gives more detail.

For notes on alternative power sources, see Chapter 8.

› Inserting a memory card

The D7200 has dual slots accepting Secure Digital (SD) cards, including high-capacity SDHC and SDXC cards.

1) Switch off the camera. If the access lamp below the multi-selector is blinking, images are being written to the card(s). Wait till it goes off.

2) Slide the card slot cover on the right side of the camera toward the rear. It will spring open.

3) To remove a memory card, press it gently into its slot; it springs out slightly. You can now remove it.

DUAL MEMORY CARD SLOTS

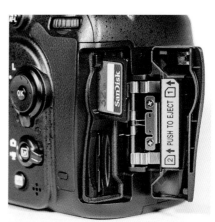

2

4) Insert a card with its label facing the rear and the "cut-off" corner facing into the slot. Gently push it into the slot until it clicks home. The access lamp will light briefly.

5) Close the card slot cover.

› Formatting a memory card

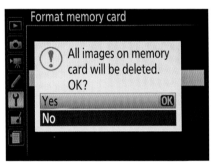

FORMATTING A MEMORY CARD IN THE SETUP MENU ⌃

You'll need to format new memory cards, or ones previously used in another camera, before use in the D7200. In everyday use, formatting is the speediest way to erase images so you can reuse the card—but make sure those images have been saved elsewhere!

You can format a card by holding down the FORMAT buttons (🗑 and ⊞) for about two seconds. A blinking **FOR** appears in the viewfinder and control panel. If both card

slots are occupied, the icon for Slot 1 will blink, and this card will be formatted first. Turn the main command dial to select Slot 2 instead. Release the buttons and press them again to format the card. Press any other button, or simply wait a few seconds, to exit without formatting.

You can also format the card through the Setup menu. This is quicker, and also makes it instantly obvious which card slot will be formatted.

› Adjusting for eyesight

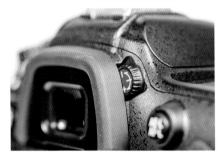

DIOPTER ADJUSTMENT DIAL ⌃

Tuning the viewfinder optics to your individual eyesight is essential for clear and comfortable viewing. The diopter adjustment dial is just right of the viewfinder. The adjustment range is between −1.7 and +0.5 m⁻¹.

Half-press the shutter-release button to activate the viewfinder readouts, then rotate the dial until they appear sharpest. If you wear glasses or contact lenses for distance vision, keep them on when adjusting the diopter, and whenever you use the viewfinder.

› Attaching the strap

Attach either end to one of the eyelets at top left and right of the camera. Loosen the strap running through the buckle, then pass the end of the strap through the eyelet and back through the buckle. Bring the end of the strap back through the buckle, between the lengths of strap already threaded (see photo). Adjust the length as required, leaving a good "tail" for security, then tighten the strap to leave it snug and tidy. Repeat on the other side.

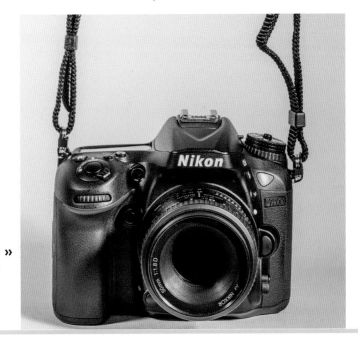

STRAP »
The strap is shown fully tightened on the left, loosely threaded on the right.

2 » BASIC OPERATION

› Mounting lenses

Switch the camera off. Remove the body cap or lens if already mounted. To remove a lens, press the lens-release button and turn the lens clockwise (as you face the front of the camera).

To mount a lens, remove its rear cap. Align the index mark on the lens with the white dot on the camera body. Insert the lens into the camera and turn it anti-clockwise until it clicks home. Do not use force; a correctly aligned lens will mount smoothly.

See Chapter 7 for information on compatible lenses.

› Controls

With strap, lens, battery, and memory card(s) on board, the D7200 is now ready to shoot.

As soon as you want to change any settings, review, or playback your shots, use Live View or shoot movies, you'll need to refer to the rear screen, or—for many but not all functions—the control panel.

Many principal camera functions are accessed through the two command dials, mode dial, and release mode dial, alone or in conjunction with various buttons. Menu navigation is principally via the multi-selector.

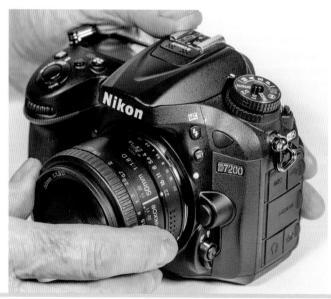

› Operating the shutter

The shutter-release button operates in two stages. Pressing it lightly, until you feel initial resistance, clears the information display, menus, or image playback (if active) and activates the metering and focus functions, making the D7200 instantly ready to shoot. Press the button more firmly (but still smoothly) to take the picture.

Warning!

Avoid touching electrical contacts on the lens or camera body. Dirty contacts can cause malfunctions.

› Switching the camera on

The power switch has three positions:
OFF The camera will not operate.
ON The camera operates normally.
☀ Move the power switch beyond **ON** and release (it will not stay in this position). This illuminates the control panel for approximately 10 seconds. Custom setting d9 allows you to keep the panel illuminated whenever the camera is active, which may be useful for night shooting but reduces battery life.

OPERATING THE SHUTTER ⌄

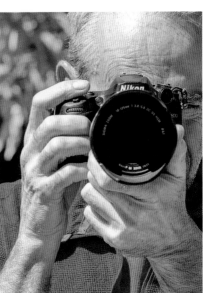

POWER SWITCH AND SHUTTER RELEASE ⌄

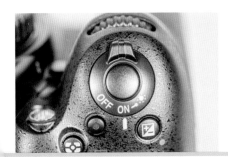

2

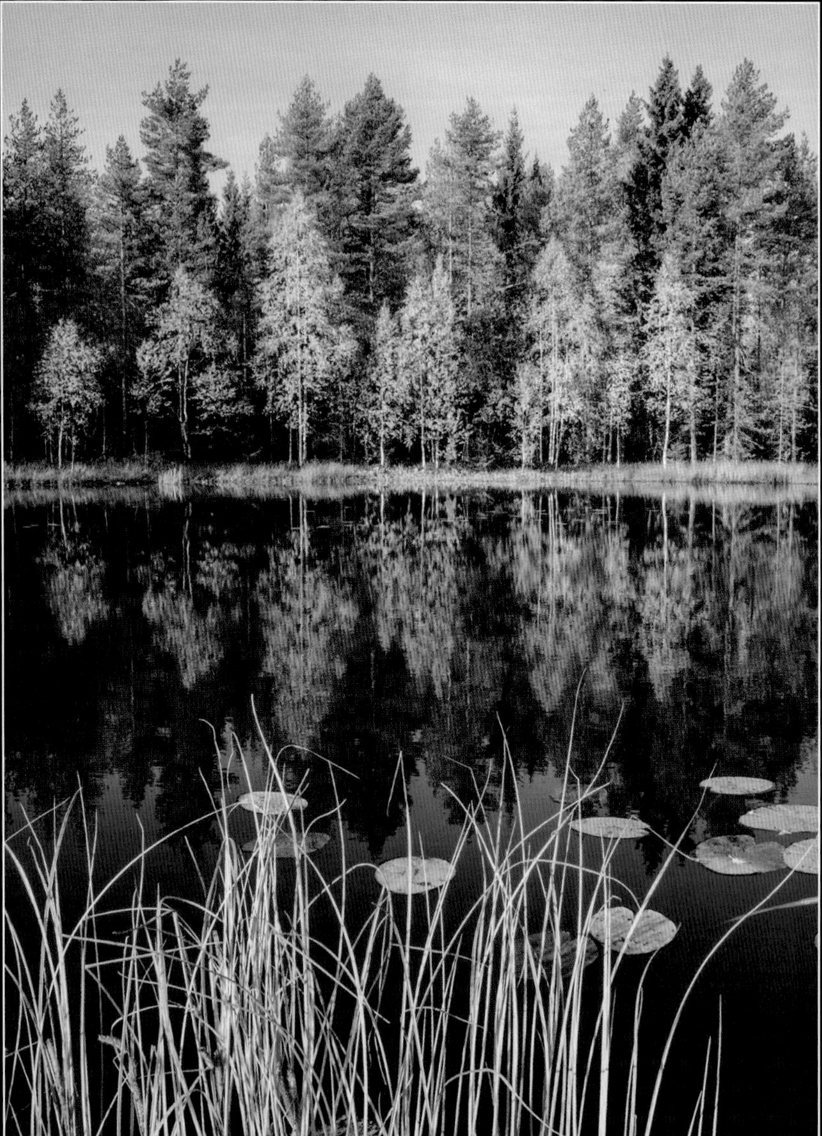

» CONTROL PANEL AND INFORMATION DISPLAY

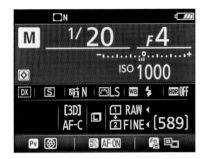

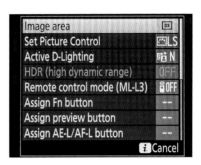

**THE INFORMATION DISPLAY ON
THE REAR LCD SCREEN** ⌃

Key shooting information is displayed in
the small control panel on top of the
camera. The same information, and more,
can be viewed in a larger form—the
information display—on the rear LCD
screen by pressing **info**. As the D7200
does not have a touchscreen, the
information display is passive: you interact
with it using buttons and dials.

› ◂🔓▸ button: quick settings

Pressing ◂🔓▸ brings up a list of key settings
(other than those which have a dedicated
button) to allow rapid access. Scroll through

DEEP WATER ««
Aperture-priority mode is ideal for control over
depth of field. In this image, I wanted everything
to be sharp from front to back.
21mm, 1/80 sec., f/14, ISO 200.

**PRESSING ◂🔓▸ ACCESSES KEY ITEMS
FROM THE CAMERA'S MENUS** ⌃

the list using the multi-selector and press
🆗 to enter the corresponding item.
    The following items are included:
Image area; **Set Picture Control**; **Active
D-Lighting**; **HDR (high dynamic range)**;
Remote control mode (ML-L3); **Assign Fn
button**; **Assign preview button**; **Assign
AE-L/AF-L button**; **Long exposure NR**;
High ISO NR.

> ### Tip
>
> *The camera provides on-screen help
> during shooting and when using
> the menus. Press* **?/o—** *to bring up
> information relating to the item
> currently selected on the screen.
> (During playback this button has
> a different function.)*

2 » COMMAND DIALS

In User-control exposure modes (**P**, **S**, **A**, and **M**), the command dials become fundamental to the operation of the Nikon D7200.

› Main command dial

In Shutter-priority or Manual mode, rotating the main command dial selects the shutter speed. In Program mode it engages program shift. In Aperture-priority mode it has no effect. In Scene and Effects modes, rotating the dial shifts between the modes.

› Sub-command dial

In Aperture-priority or Manual mode, rotating the sub-command dial selects the aperture. In Shutter-priority or Program mode it has no effect.

› Uses with control buttons

The command dials are also used in conjunction with various control buttons to change key settings (see table opposite): hold down the button and rotate the dial to make a selection. It's possible to change most of these using the menus instead, but using a button and dial is faster and soon becomes intuitive.

More functions can be added, as the dials can also be used in conjunction with the Fn, Preview (Pv), and **AE-L/AF-L** buttons. You can choose which functions these perform through Custom Settings f2, f3, and f4 (see pages 122–125).

THE SUB-COMMAND DIAL ☒

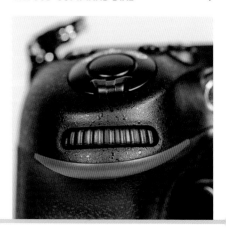

THE MAIN COMMAND DIAL ☒

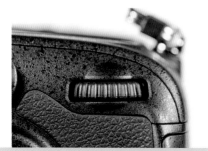

Principal uses of the command dials in conjunction with control buttons

Command dial	Other button	Function
Main	⊞	Select the level of exposure compensation
Main	⚡	Select the flash mode
Sub	⚡	Select the level of flash compensation
Main	⊕	Select the image quality
Sub	⊕	Select the image size
Main	⊙	Select AF mode
Sub	⊙	Select AF-area mode
Main	⊝▦	Select the ISO sensitivity
Sub	⊝▦	Toggle Auto-ISO sensitivity control on/off
Main	?/○┓	Select the white balance setting
Sub	?/○┓	Select white balance preset

› Multi-selector

The multi-selector, on the camera back, is also an important part of the control system. Its primary use when shooting is in selecting the focus point. It is also used to navigate through images in playback, and when navigating the menus. The ⊛ button at its center is used to confirm settings.

The collar around the multi-selector has an L (Lock) position. When locked, the multi-selector can still be used for playback and menu navigation, but the focus point cannot be moved. To allow focus point selection, move the collar to the unlocked position (white dot).

MULTI-SELECTOR ⌄

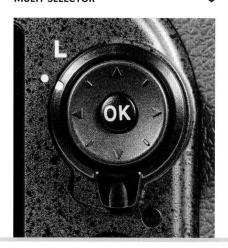

2 » RELEASE MODE

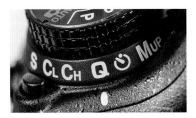

The release mode dial has six possible positions. To prevent accidental switching between release modes the dial has a lock button. Depress this to allow the dial to rotate.

THE RELEASE MODE DIAL SET 　　　　**«**
TO QUIET MODE

RELEASE MODE OPTIONS

Setting	Description
S Single Frame	The camera takes a single shot each time the shutter release is fully depressed.
C_L Continuous Low speed	The camera fires continuously as long as the shutter release is fully depressed. The default frame rate is 3fps but this can be varied between 1 and 6fps using Custom Setting d5.
C_H Continuous High speed	The camera fires continuously at the maximum possible frame rate as long as the shutter release is fully depressed.
Q Quiet mode	Shoot as normal but there are no alert beeps and the mirror-return after each shot is damped to provide a quieter release.
⟳ Self-timer	The shutter is released a set interval after the release button is depressed. Can be used to minimize camera shake and for self-portraits. The default interval is 10 sec. but 2 sec., 5 sec., or 20 sec. can be set using Custom Setting c3.
M_{UP} Mirror-up	The mirror is raised when the shutter release is fully depressed; press again to take the picture. Useful to minimize vibration caused by "mirror slap", but now superseded in many circumstances by Live View mode.

RIDING HIGH

I used single-frame release mode here, relying on timing to catch the moment when the front wheel was off the ground. *24mm, 1/800 sec., f/7.1, ISO 200.*

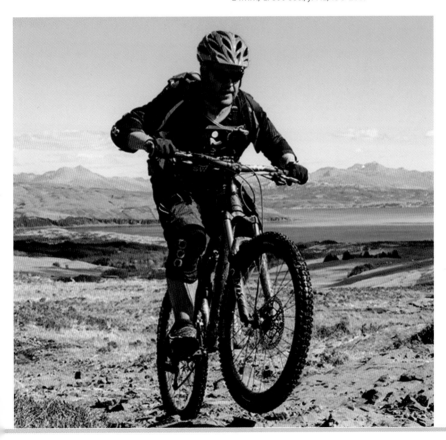

The maximum shooting rate for all file formats is around 6 frames per second (fps), rising to 7fps when you engage 1.3x crop mode. The maximum rate is not always attainable—any difficulty in focusing can slow things down, as can the use of slower shutter speeds. The speed of the memory cards can also be a factor (see below).

RIVER CROSSING ⹝
Action shooting should be about timing, rather than firing off lots of shots indiscriminately.
42mm, 1/500 sec., f/8, ISO 400.

› Buffer

Images are held in the camera's internal memory ("buffer") until they can be written to the memory card. Usually you'll never notice any delay, but when you shoot images in a continuous burst you can fill up the buffer. How soon this happens depends on factors including image quality and size and the speed of the memory card.

The maximum number of frames you can shoot in a burst at current settings is shown in the viewfinder at bottom right

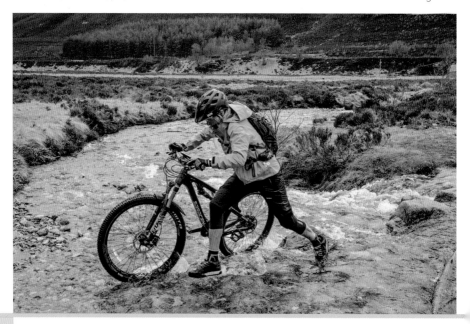

when you half-press the shutter release. e.g. **[r12]**. **(0)** means that the buffer is full; no more shots can be taken until enough data has been transferred to the memory card to free up buffer capacity. This normally only happens if you're shooting in a continuous release mode (Cн or Cʟ), and results in a slow-down or a break in the rhythm of the shutter.

When Image quality is set to JPEG, you can shoot 100 shots continuously at 6fps, at least with a fast memory card—I've verified this with 80Mb/s memory cards.

Buffer limits are much tighter when shooting RAW. If **NEF (RAW) recording** is set to **12-bit**, the limit is about 20 shots before shooting speed slows dramatically; if you change the setting to **14-bit** the maximum rate drops to around 4.5fps and the burst limit at this rate to about 12 shots. Again, I've tested this with 80Mb/s memory cards.

In practice, these buffer/burst limits are rarely a serious handicap. Even when shooting fast action, I very rarely feel the need to shoot more than a handful of frames in one burst. I do set **NEF (RAW) recording** to 12-bit for action shooting, but I'd still rather shoot RAW than JPEG.

Tip

Shooting lots of long continuous bursts isn't necessarily the best way to capture the peak of the action— but it certainly does leave you with an awful lot of images to edit later.

QUICK BURST ⍒
I shot a burst of four frames when the runner was at the right distance from the camera.
200mm, 1/640 sec., f/4, ISO 400.

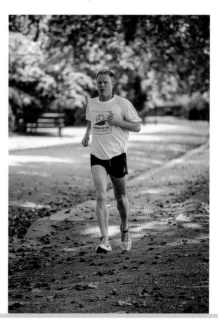

2 » EXPOSURE MODES

Exposure modes, selected from the mode dial, are fundamental to the camera's operation and the choice of exposure mode makes a significant difference to the amount of control you can—or can't—exercise. The D7200's mode dial is provided with a lock: press the button at the center of the dial to release it, then rotate it to the required position.

The D7200 has a very wide choice of exposure modes, but they fall conveniently into three main groups: Full Auto modes, Scene modes, and User-control modes. User-control modes give you complete freedom to control virtually everything on the camera.

In Full Auto and Scene modes, by contrast, the majority of settings are determined automatically, including basic shooting settings, whether flash can be used, and how the camera processes the shot. Full Auto modes use generalized settings that aim to cover most eventualities while Scene mode settings are tailored to particular shooting scenarios. There is some scope to override the automatic choices: typically, you can change the ISO setting, and in modes which automatically activate the flash you can turn it off. Still, most settings are out of your hands.

The mode dial has three extra positions, U1, U2, and EFFECTS. U1 and U2 allow instant access to predetermined User settings. EFFECTS gives access to a range of stylized image effects.

MODE DIAL ⌄

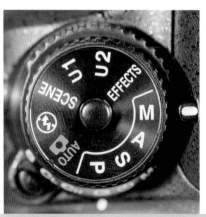

MODE GROUP	EXPOSURE MODE	
Full Auto modes	AUTO Auto Auto (flash off)	Leaves all decisions about settings to the camera.
Scene modes (set mode dial to SCENE and use main dial to select)	Portrait Landscape Child Sports Close up Night portrait Night landscape Party/indoor Beach/snow Sunset Dusk/dawn Pet portrait Candlelight Blossom Autumn colors Food	Choose the Scene mode to suit the subject and the camera then employs appropriate settings.
Special Effects modes (set mode dial to EFFECTS and use information display)	Night Vision Color sketch Miniature Effect Selective Color Silhouette High key Lo Low key	Use for more extreme pictorial effects.
User-control modes	P Program S Shutter-priority A Aperture-priority M Manual	Allows full control over the entire range of camera settings.

Nikon calls these "point-and-shoot" modes, which is a fair reflection of how they're likely to be used. Left to its own devices in these modes, the camera will capture acceptable shots under most conditions, but results may not always exactly match what you had in mind. They're okay for snapshots, but stifle creativity, and limit the D7200's potential.

There's one difference between the two modes. In ⬛ᴬᵁᵀᴼ **Auto** mode the built-in flash will automatically pop up and fire if the camera determines light levels are too low. You can turn it off, but it's easier just to switch to ⚡.

In ⚡ **Auto (flash off)** mode the flash stays off at all times. This is useful in situations where flash is banned or would be intrusive, or when you just want to discover what the D7200 can do in low light (which is a lot!).

Taking the picture

Basic picture-taking is essentially the same in all Full Auto and Scene modes.

1) Select the exposure mode by rotating the mode dial to the appropriate position; for scene modes, set it to SCENE and then use the information display and main command dial as described on page 40.

2) Frame the picture.

3) Half-depress the release button to activate focusing and exposure. The focus

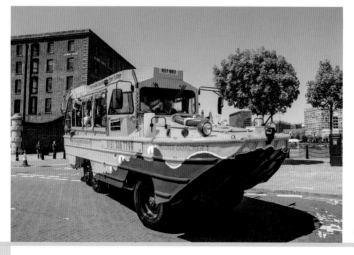

FULL AUTO MODE «
Full auto mode is ideal when shots need to be grabbed quickly, but can diminish the sense of control and creativity. *18mm, 1/500 sec., f/11, ISO 200.*

point(s) will be displayed in the viewfinder image, and shutter speed and aperture settings will appear at the bottom of the viewfinder screen.

5) Fully depress the shutter release to take the picture.

Exposure warnings
In all modes except Manual, if the camera detects that light levels are too low or, more rarely, too high for an acceptable exposure, a warning will be displayed in both the viewfinder and the information display. The exposure indicators in the viewfinder flash on and off. If it's too dark, a flash symbol also blinks. Similar warnings appear in the information display if it is on.

The camera will still take pictures under these conditions but results may be underexposed or subject to camera shake (assuming the warning arises because it's too dark). Possible solutions include using flash, adjusting the ISO sensitivity, or fitting a different lens with a wider maximum aperture.

BUSKER »
Auto (flash off) mode is suitable when flash is banned or—as in this case—it could cause disturbance. *125mm, 1/200 sec., f/5.6, ISO 100.*

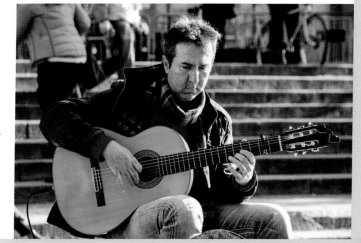

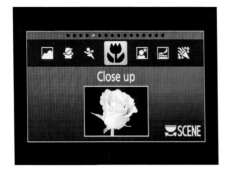

SCENE MODE SELECTION ⌃

Scene modes are a quick way to set the camera for shooting in particular situations. They can also be a first step to exploring a wider range of options on the D7200.

To select a scene mode, set the mode dial to SCENE. Rotate the main command dial and the monitor scrolls through the available modes, with the current mode's icon highlighted. (If this screen does not appear, press **info** to activate the information display.) The mode's name also appears, with

a thumbnail image illustrating an appropriate subject. This selection screen disappears after a few seconds, but the mode icon remains in the top left corner of the information display.

Switching between Scene modes naturally affects basic shooting parameters like how the camera focuses and how it sets shutter speed and aperture. The modes also determine how the camera processes the image (at least for JPEG images). For instance, Nikon Picture Control settings are predetermined. In 🧍 Portrait mode, for example, the camera applies a Portrait Picture Control for natural colors and flattering skin tones. Most Scene modes also employ Auto white balance, but in some cases the white balance setting is predetermined to suit specific subjects.

In some Scene modes, the built-in flash will automatically activate if the camera determines light levels are too low. You can turn it off fairly easily (hold 🗲 and rotate the main command dial until the (🗲) icon appears in the control panel/information display). Alternatively, attaching a separate flashgun will override the built-in unit—and usually improves results dramatically (see page 156).

In other Scene modes, the built-in flash remains off regardless of the light level. However, if you attach a separate flashgun this will operate normally. Otherwise, if you want flash, switch to a different mode.

Tip

If you regularly use one or two particular Scene modes, you could assign these to positions U1 and U2 on the mode dial. This then becomes the quickest way to select these modes.

› Using Scene modes

Some experienced photographers may be dismissive of Scene modes, but there's no doubt that they have real value both as part of the learning process and as a very quick way to set the camera appropriately when time is at a premium.

Scene modes also allow you to override the automatic settings in several ways. This makes them more versatile and can offer another step along the learning curve. The more you use these overrides, the closer

LANDSCAPE MODE ⌄
Landscape mode aims for vibrant colors and good depth of field.

Tip

Don't feel too limited by the title of the mode. Some lend themselves to other applications too. For example, as there's no separate "wildlife" mode, Sports mode is often a good choice, especially when shooting distant creatures with long lenses. Food mode can be used for all kinds of close-up subjects when you don't want to use flash.

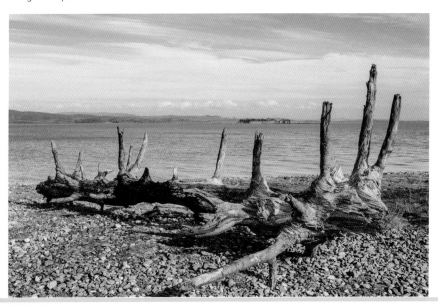

DEFAULT SETTINGS FOR SCENE MODES

Scene mode	AF mode	AF-area mode	White balance	Flash mode
Portrait	AF-A	Auto-area AF	Auto1	Auto
Landscape	AF-A	Auto-area AF	Auto1	Off
Child	AF-A	Auto-area AF	Auto1	Auto
Sports	AF-A	51-point dynamic area	Auto1	Off
Close up	AF-S	Single-area AF	Auto1	Auto
Night portrait	AF-A	Auto-area AF	Auto2	Auto slow sync
Night landscape	AF-A	Auto-area AF	Auto2	Off
Party/indoor	AF-A	Auto-area AF	Auto2	Auto with red-eye reduction
Beach/snow	AF-A	Auto-area AF	Auto1	Off
Sunset	AF-A	Auto-area AF	Direct sunlight	Off
Dusk/dawn	AF-A	Auto-area AF	Preset	Off
Pet portrait	AF-A	51-point dynamic area	Auto1	Auto
Candlelight	AF-A	Single-area AF	Preset	Off
Blossom	AF-A	Auto-area AF	Auto1	Off
Autumn colors	AF-A	Auto-area AF	Auto1	Off
Food	AF-A	Single-area AF	Auto1	Manual

Picture Control	Notes
Portrait	Camera sets wide aperture to reduce depth of field.
Landscape	Camera sets small aperture to increase depth of field. This can lead to slow shutter speeds: a tripod may be needed.
Standard	Camera sets wide aperture to reduce depth of field, but uses higher shutter speeds than ⚇ as subjects may be more active.
Standard	Camera sets fast shutter speed to freeze movement, usually leading to wide aperture and therefore shallow depth of field.
Standard	Camera sets medium to small aperture to improve depth of field, often leading to slow shutter speeds: a tripod may be needed.
Portrait	In low ambient light, camera sets long shutter speed to record an image of the background. Tripod often needed.
Standard	Allows long exposures (up to 30 sec.). Tripod usually required. Long Exposure noise reduction often applies, leading to delay before another shot can be taken.
Standard	Gives shorter exposure times than ▨ , so more suitable for handheld shooting. Red-eye reduction flash creates noticeable shutter delay.
Landscape	Exposure compensation may be applied automatically to preserve bright tones.
Landscape	Long exposures are common. Tripod often required.
Landscape	Long exposures very common. Tripod usually required.
Standard	Generally similar to ⚇ Child, but AF-assist illuminator turns off.
Standard	Long exposures very common. Tripod usually required. Portrait subjects need to keep still.
Landscape	Employs Active D-Lighting to retain detail in highlight areas.
Vivid	Tripod sometimes needed.
Standard	Built-in flash can be used but not recommended as it produces ugly shadows at close range.

you approach the experience offered by the User-control modes.

There are some things you can't override, notably the white balance and Picture Control settings. However, if you shoot RAW, even these aren't locked in to the final image. You also can't access Active D-Lighting or HDR (high dynamic range) options.

› Overrides

In all Scene modes you can access the full range of image quality, area, and size options, notably the ability to shoot RAW.

In all Scene modes, ISO is controlled automatically by default but you can always override it by pressing **ISO** and rotating the main command dial.

In all Scene modes you can override the default focusing settings by pressing ⊙ and rotating the main command dial (to set AF mode) or the sub-command dial (to set AF-area mode).

Flash options

In some Scene modes (see table on previous page), the built-in flash activates automatically if the camera deems light

PET PORTRAIT MODE ⌄⌄
It's not exactly a pet, but Pet portrait mode still works well here.

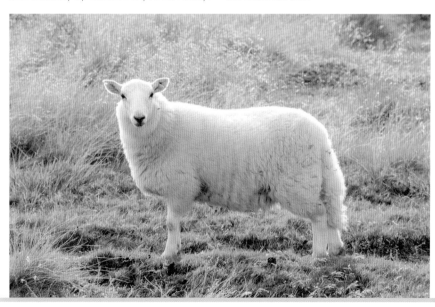

levels too low. You can turn it off if necessary, by pressing ⚡ and rotating the main command dial until the (⚡) icon appears in the information display. Alternatively, attaching a separate flashgun will override the built-in unit, and often improves results dramatically (see page 156). You can also select other flash modes, or set flash compensation.

In other Scene modes, the built-in flash remains off regardless of the light level. Here you can't change settings to override this, but if you attach a separate flashgun it will operate normally.

There's one anomaly: in 🍴 Food, the built-in flash does not operate automatically but can be activated

manually with ⚡. (However, think twice about using flash in a restaurant, as you'll probably irritate other diners.)

› Exposure options

You can't directly set aperture or shutter speed, and you can't bracket exposures, but you can use exposure compensation and exposure lock.

FOOD MODE ⌄
In food mode, the flash does not activate automatically, and I left it off for this shot.

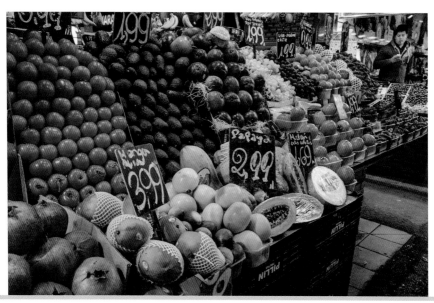

» SPECIAL EFFECTS MODES

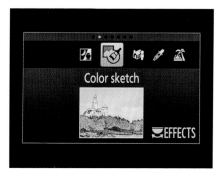

EFFECTS MODE SELECTION ⌃

Special Effects modes are like "extreme" Scene modes, producing striking effects through a combination of shooting settings and image processing. They can be used in Live View or Movie mode. Some similar effects can also be applied to images through the Retouch menu.

Most Effects modes produce JPEG images. If Image Quality is set to RAW, the camera creates a Fine JPEG image instead. Exceptions are ⛰, ⊞, and Lo, which can deliver RAW images.

Live View gives an approximate preview of the effect. For some modes, like ✐, this is essential. In ⬚ and ⬚, shooting in Live View/movie lets you modify the effect.

> **Using Special Effects modes**

Selecting Special Effects modes is just like selecting Scene modes, except of course that you start by setting the mode dial to EFFECTS instead.

In Live View, **OK SET** appears at the bottom of the screen if the current mode offers shooting/processing options; press ⊛ to choose options.

The following modes are available:

⚅ Night Vision

Uses extreme high ISO settings (maximum Hi BW2 or ISO 102,400); produces monochrome images. In very low light levels, manual focus may be required. No options.

⬚ Color Sketch

Turns a photo into something resembling a colored pencil drawing. Movies can be recorded; the Nikon manual says they play back like a slide show or series of stills but I haven't found this to be true. There are options for **Vividness** and **Outlines**.

⬚ Miniature Effect

Mimics the recent fad for shooting images with extremely small and localized depth of field, making real scenes look like miniature models. Movie clips play back at high speed. Live View options: use multi-selector to reposition the in-focus zone.

✎ Selective Color

Select particular color(s); other hues are rendered in monochrome. Colors are selected in Live View (select the color under the focus point by pressing ▲).

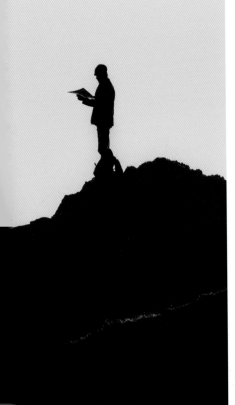

Silhouette

The camera's metering favors bright backgrounds such as vivid skies; foreground subjects record as silhouettes. Most effective for subjects with interesting outlines. No options.

High key

Produces images filled with light tones, usually with no blacks or deep tones at all, apparently by a combination of exposure compensation and Active D-Lighting. No options.

Lo Low key

Low key is basically the opposite, creating a deep, low-toned image. You can achieve a similar (but more controllable) result using exposure compensation. No options.

SILHOUETTE «
Silhouette mode can be very effective when used for the right subject.

The remaining four modes are traditional standards, which will be familiar to any experienced photographer.

It's these modes that really allow you to harness the full power of the D7200. As well as allowing direct control over the basic settings of aperture and shutter speed (even in **P** mode, through flexible program), these modes give you free rein to employ controls like white balance, Active D-Lighting, and Nikon Picture Controls. These give you lots of influence over the look and feel of the image. You can also select different metering modes for finer control over exposure. You can exploit HDR (high dynamic range) imaging, shoot multiple exposures and, at least in manual mode, use shutter speeds longer than 30 seconds.

› (P) Programmed auto

In **P** mode the camera sets a combination of shutter speed and aperture that will give correctly exposed results in most situations.

IN CONTROL ❖
User-control modes give me the feeling that I'm in charge and that the final result will be exactly what I'm aiming for.
34mm, 1/320 sec., f/13, ISO 200.

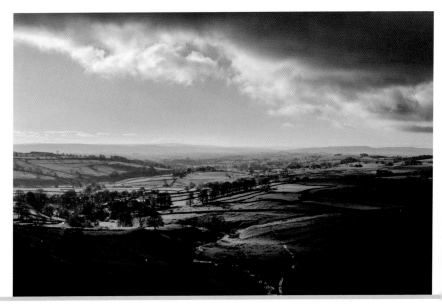

The same is true of Full Auto modes and Scene modes, but **P** mode offers several ways to modify these exposure settings, including flexible program (below), exposure lock, and exposure compensation. It also gives complete freedom to adjust other parameters such as white balance.

Flexible program

In **P** mode, you can vary the permutations of shutter speed and aperture by rotating the command dial (flexible program). This does not change the overall exposure (make the picture darker or lighter): use exposure compensation for that. Instead, flexible program shifts the balance between shutter speed and aperture. You can see them change in the displays.

This is a quick way to achieve practically the same direct control over aperture/shutter speed offered by (**S**) Shutter-priority or (**A**) Aperture-priority modes.

When flexible program is in effect the **P** indicator in the displays changes to **P***.

PROGRAM   ⌄
P mode allows a quick response but also lets you tailor camera settings to suit your own creative ideas.
20mm, 1/60 sec., f/8, ISO 250.

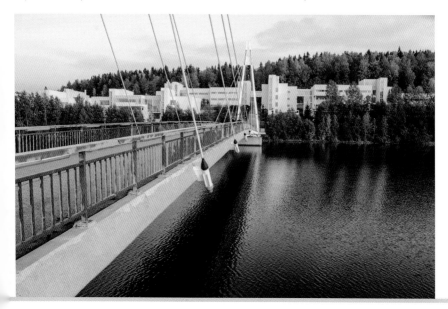

› (S) Shutter-priority auto

In Shutter-priority mode, you control the shutter speed using the main command dial, and the camera sets an appropriate aperture for correctly exposed results. You can set shutter speeds between 30 sec. and 1/8000 sec. You can fine-tune exposure through exposure lock, exposure compensation, or exposure bracketing.

Significance of shutter speed

Shutter speed is significant mainly as it affects how motion is recorded. In essence, fast shutter speeds tend to freeze motion, while slower ones are more likely to record it with a degree of blur. This applies both in relation to movement of your subject and to movement of the camera itself. Intentional camera movement and/or use of controlled blur, as in panning shots, can create very effective results. (Sports mode does not cater for this approach.)

On the other hand, unintentional movement, usually termed camera shake, can ruin a shot. Using faster shutter speeds is one strategy which can help us avoid or minimize the effects of camera shake.

Movement is not just a concern for sports and wildlife specialists. For example, it can be an issue in portraits (especially of children and animals). Even in apparently static landscapes, movement is often present, whether it's scudding clouds, running water, or foliage swaying in the breeze.

> **Note:**
> Shutter-priority auto is not available with older lenses lacking a CPU. If a non-CPU lens is attached, the camera will switch to Aperture-priority mode. The **S** indicator in the control panel will blink and **A** will be displayed in the viewfinder. Much the same applies in **P** mode.

FALLING WATER »
I set the slowest shutter speed possible under the conditions to smooth out the appearance of the water. A neutral density filter would have allowed me to set an even slower speed. *85mm, 1 sec., f/22, ISO 100, tripod.*

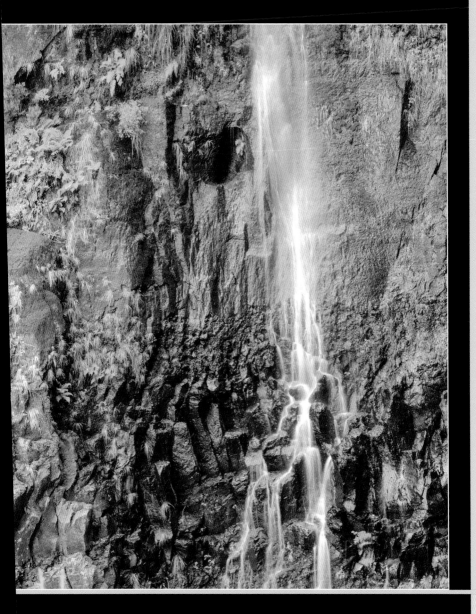

› (A) Aperture-priority auto

In Aperture-priority (**A**) mode, you control the aperture using the sub-command dial, and the camera sets an appropriate shutter speed to give correctly exposed results.

The range of apertures you can set is determined by the lens that's fitted. You can fine-tune exposure, as usual, through exposure lock, compensation, or bracketing.

Significance of aperture

Aperture is principally significant as one of the key factors influencing depth of field. Depth of field describes the zone in front of and behind the actual point of focus, in which objects appear to be sharp in the final image. The other main factors determining depth of field are the focal length of the lens and the distance to the subject.

Sometimes a shallow depth of field is exactly what you want, as it makes the subject stand out against a soft background. For other images you may want to try and have everything sharp from front to back—this is the traditional (but not compulsory!) approach in landscape photography, for instance.

For more about depth of field and how to preview it, see page 80.

> **Note:**
> Aperture-priority auto is available with older lenses lacking a CPU. For best results with such lenses, enter the maximum aperture of the lens via **Non-CPU lens data** in the Setup menu.

THROUGH THE REEDS »

I focused on the reeds in the foreground and allowed the background to go soft. This puts the emphasis on the strong forms of the reeds, while giving an overall impression of the setting. *21mm, 1/80 sec., f/14, ISO 200.*

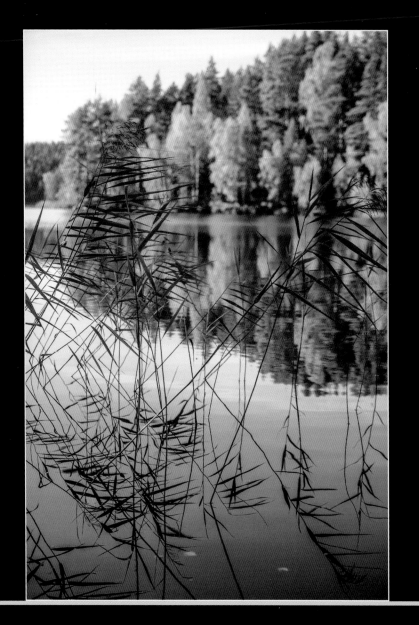

2

› (M) Manual

In **M** mode, you control both shutter speed (with the main command dial) and aperture (with the sub-command dial). Manual mode suits a considered approach, especially when time is not too pressing. Many photographers use it habitually to retain complete control.

NIGHT SCENE ⌄

If there's no cable release to hand, the T setting is the best bet when exposures longer than 30 sec. are required.

16mm, 44 sec., f/22, ISO 100, tripod.

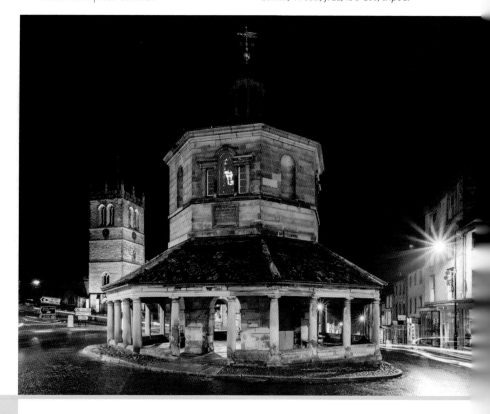

The range of apertures that you can set is determined by the lens that's fitted. Shutter speeds can be set between 30 sec. and 1/8000 sec., as in shutter-priority, but manual mode offers two additional options, B and T (see below). These are the only ways to achieve exposures longer than 30 seconds, which are desirable, if not essential, for fireworks displays, moonlit landscapes, star trails, and many other subjects. You'll need a tripod or other solid camera support.

B (Bulb)

Rotate the main command dial until **Bulb** appears in viewfinder, control panel, and information display.

In Bulb mode, the shutter remains open as long as the shutter-release button is held down. However, holding it down with your finger is tedious and uncomfortable, and can cause camera shake. It's advisable to use a remote control of some kind (see Chapter 8 Accessories and care).

Exposures longer than 30 minutes are only possible in B.

T (Time)

Rotate the main command dial until **Time** appears in the information display. The viewfinder and control panel show two dashes. Press and release the shutter button—the shutter remains open, either until you press the button again or until 30 minutes have elapsed.

The exposure meter gives no reading when B or T are set. Sometimes the only way to get the exposure right is by trial and error. This can, of course, be a long-winded process. Check the battery has plenty of juice before essaying any really long exposures.

Using the Analog exposure displays

In Manual mode, an analog exposure display appears in the center of the viewfinder readouts and in the information display. This shows whether the photograph would be under- or overexposed at current settings.

To match exposure to the camera's recommendation, adjust shutter speed and/or aperture until the indicator is aligned with the *0* in the center of the display. The resulting exposure will generally be correct, but if time allows you can review the image and check the histogram display (see Playback, page 98) after taking a shot. If necessary, make further adjustments for creative effect or to achieve a specific result.

2 » ISO SENSITIVITY SETTINGS

ISO sensitivity settings govern the sensor's response to greater or lesser amounts of light. The wide ISO ranges of digital cameras—especially those with larger sensors, like DSLRs—are among their greatest features. In the bad old days of film, once you'd loaded a roll of film, you were stuck with the same ISO for 36 exposures. If light levels changed significantly, it could be a real struggle to maintain a usable aperture and shutter speed. Now, all three factors are continually variable. This is truly liberating.

At higher ISO settings, less light is needed to capture an acceptable image. Higher ISO settings are also useful when you need a small aperture for increased depth of field or a fast shutter speed to freeze rapid movement. Conversely, lower ISO settings are useful in brighter conditions, and/or when you require wide apertures or slow shutter speeds.

The D7200 offers ISO settings from 100 to 25,600. There are two further settings, but these only allow black-and-white JPEG images to be captured. **Hi BW1** is equivalent to 51,200 ISO and **Hi BW2** to 102,400 ISO. These values are often employed when using 🎴 Night Vision mode.

INDOOR ISO
A high ISO setting enabled me to catch this shot in a dimly lit pub without flash.
80mm, 1/20 sec., f/5, ISO 12,800.

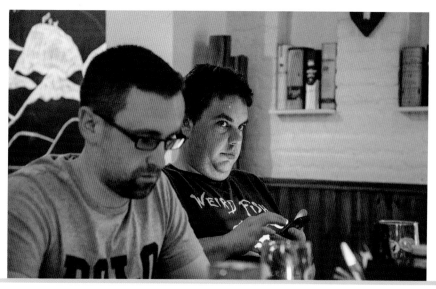

› Noise

Image noise appears as random speckles of varying brightness or color. It's most obtrusive in areas that should have an even tone, especially in darker parts of the image. The D7200 generally produces clean images with low noise, but—as with all cameras—noise increases noticeably at higher ISO settings. At some point, especially if you're viewing on a large screen or making large prints, noise levels may exceed your tolerance.

However, viewing at 100% on a large screen makes noise (and any other tiny flaws in the image) all too obvious. Such "pixel peeping" is not normal viewing and images may still be perfectly acceptable for full-screen viewing and small or medium-sized prints. Experiment with a range of settings to see what level of image noise is acceptable for your needs.

> ### Tip
>
> *By default, **Hi BW1** and **Hi BW2** can't be set with ⊖▦ and the main command dial, only through the Photo Shooting menu.*

› Setting the ISO

The normal way to set the ISO is by pressing ⊖▦ and rotating the main command dial until you see the desired setting in the displays. Alternatively, use **ISO sensitivity settings** in the Photo Shooting menu.

Then there's **Easy ISO**, enabled via Custom setting d8. This lets you set ISO simply by rotating the main command dial (in Aperture-priority mode) or sub-command dial (in Shutter-priority or Program mode). It does not apply in other modes.

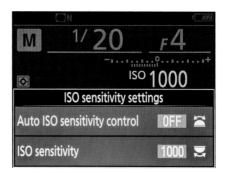

ISO DIALOG IN THE INFORMATION DISPLAY ⌃

2

› Auto ISO

It's important to understand that the D7200 offers two flavors of Auto ISO. In Full Auto, Scene, and Effects modes, ISO setting is normally fully automatic. (However, in almost all these modes, except 🏃, you can change to a manual setting simply by pressing ✋ and rotating the main command dial.)

In **P, S, A**, and **M** modes, Auto ISO—full name now **Auto ISO sensitivity control**— means something different; it's more of a failsafe. You still set the ISO manually, but

Auto ISO sensitivity control allows the D7200 to deviate from the selected ISO if this becomes necessary to maintain correct exposure. For example, if you are using Shutter-priority with a shutter speed of 1/1000 sec. and an ISO setting of 100,

SEEING THE LIGHT ⌄
I used the base ISO setting to maximize dynamic range. This is a single RAW file, with no HDR trickery involved.
18mm, 1/40 sec., f/11, ISO 100.

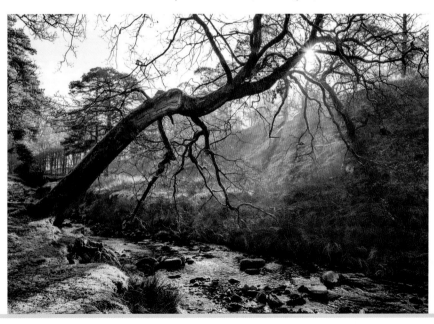

prevailing light levels may not allow correct exposure within the aperture range available on the lens. The camera will then adjust the ISO setting until it can achieve acceptable exposure at an available aperture.

Auto ISO sensitivity control is off by default and must be enabled through the **ISO sensitivity settings** item in the Photo Shooting menu, using the **Auto ISO sensitivity control** submenu. This has further options.

Hi ISO command dial access
Turn this **On** to allow you to access **Hi BW1** and **Hi BW2** settings with ⊖▒ and the main command dial.

Maximum sensitivity
Use this to limit the maximum ISO which the camera can employ when applying Auto ISO sensitivity control. For instance, if you feel that image noise becomes unacceptable above ISO 3200, you can set this as the upper limit.

Minimum shutter speed
This lets you set a shutter speed limit below which the camera will not go. This only applies in **P** and **A** modes; in **S** and **M** modes the camera will continue to use the

shutter speed you set. This submenu includes an **Auto** option; within this you can make a choice along a scale from **Slower** to **Faster**. If you err towards Faster, the camera will increase the ISO more quickly to maintain higher shutter speeds. The camera takes focal length into account; longer lenses require higher shutter speeds to avoid camera shake. If you use a range of focal lengths, the flexibility offered by the Auto option is appealing.

AUTO-ISO ⌄
Using the Auto-ISO option can mean one less thing to worry about when shooting. *200mm, 1/800 sec., f/5.6, ISO 100.*

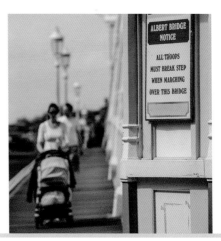

2 » METERING MODES

To ensure that images are correctly exposed, the camera must measure the light levels; this is known as exposure metering. The D7200 provides three different metering modes, which should cover any eventuality. Switch between them using the ⚏ button and main command dial (this is only possible in User-control modes—in other modes matrix metering is permanently selected).

› ▣ 3D Color Matrix Metering II

Using a 2016-pixel color sensor, 3D Color Matrix Metering II analyzes data on the brightness, color, and contrast of the scene. If a Type G, D, or E Nikkor lens is fitted, the system also analyzes distance information, based on where the camera focuses— hence "3D". With other lenses, distance

METERING MODE BUTTON　　　　　　　⌄

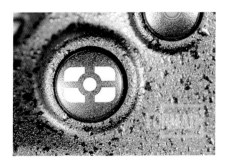

information is not used and metering reverts to a non-3D version.

Matrix metering is recommended for the vast majority of shooting and will generally produce accurate results.

› ⦿ Center-weighted metering

In this very traditional metering method, the camera meters the entire frame, but gives predominance to a central circle approximately 8mm across. Center-weighted metering can be useful, for example, in portraiture, where the key subject usually occupies the central portion of the frame (although 🏃 Portrait mode sticks with matrix metering).

› ⦿ Spot metering

The camera meters solely from a smaller (3.5mm) area. With a CPU lens, this area centers on the current focus point. With a non-CPU lens, or if ▬ Auto-area AF is in use, the metering point is the center of the frame.

For advanced users, spot metering can be an extremely powerful tool, for example, where an important subject is very much darker or lighter than the background. Matrix metering is more likely to compromise between subject and background.

METERING CHOICES

There's a very wide brightness range here. I could have spot-metered the brightest cloud and deepest shadow, but instead I took a test shot and assessed the results using the histogram and highlights displays.
23mm, 1/50 sec., f/11, ISO 100.

Tip

To be honest, I almost never use anything but matrix metering. In taking charge of exposure, my advice is to concentrate on mastering the histogram first. This is the best tool for judging exposure, especially when shooting RAW. Whatever metering method you use, you can always override its recommendation (e.g. using exposure compensation) if you don't like the results.

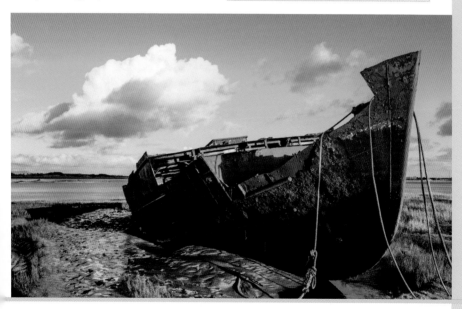

» EXPOSURE COMPENSATION

The D7200 will deliver accurate exposures under most conditions, but no camera is infallible. Nor can it read your mind or anticipate your creative ideas. Sometimes it needs a little help to get the result spot-on. Exposure compensation is one way to do this. Alternatives are exposure bracketing and exposure lock.

The principle is simple: to make the image lighter (to keep light tones looking light), increase exposure, and use positive compensation. Conversely, to keep dark tones looking dark, use negative compensation. You can check after shooting and make further adjustments if necessary; here the highlights display and especially the histogram are extremely helpful.

Exposure compensation is available in **P**, **S**, **A**, and Scene modes, plus 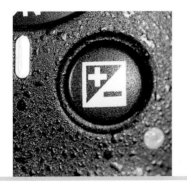 Night Vision. In Auto and other Effects modes exposure compensation is not available.

EXPOSURE COMPENSATION BUTTON ⌄

> ### Tips
>
> *Shooting RAW certainly gives extra room for recovery in post-processing, but to ensure the best capture of detail in both shadows and highlights it's still best to aim for accurate exposure in the first place.*
>
> *In M mode ⊡ sets aperture, and you "compensate" instead by adjusting shutter speed, aperture, and/or ISO until the analog display shows a + or – value.*

> ### Using Exposure compensation

Exposure compensation can be set between –5 Ev and +5 Ev, though you'll rarely need these extremes. It can be applied in steps of ⅓ Ev (default) or ½ Ev, depending on the option selected for Custom setting b1.

1) Press ⊡ and rotate the command dial to set negative or positive compensation. The chosen value is shown in the information display, control panel, and viewfinder.

2) Release ⊡ .

3) Take the picture as usual. If possible, check that the result is satisfactory.

4) To reset exposure compensation, repeat step 1 until the value returns to *0.0*. Otherwise, compensation will apply to later shots which don't need it. It does not reset automatically even when the camera is switched off.

› Exposure bracketing

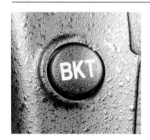

EXPOSURE BRACKETING BUTTON ⌃

1) Select the type of bracketing required using Custom setting e6. Select **AE only** to ensure that only exposure values are varied. (If flash is not active, **AE & Flash** has the same effect.)

2) Hold **BKT** and rotate the main command dial to select the number of shots (**2**, **3**, **5**, **7**, or **9**) required for the bracketing sequence.

3) Still holding **BKT**, rotate the

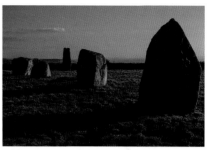

−1 Ev

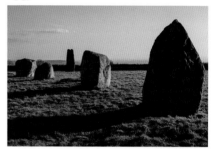

0 Ev

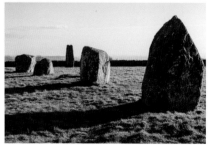

+1 Ev

STANDING STONES ⌃
42mm, 1/320 sec./1/160 sec./1/80 sec., f/11, ISO 100, tripod.

sub-command dial to select the exposure increment between each shot in the sequence. Possible values are: **0.3**, **0.7**, **1**, **2**, or **3** Ev.

4) Frame, focus, and shoot normally. The camera varies the exposure for each frame until the sequence is completed. In Cʜ or Cʟ release mode, shooting will pause at this point even if you keep the shutter release depressed.

Tips

Using exposure bracketing while shooting moving subjects is a lottery: the frame with the best exposure may not coincide with the subject being in the best position. Ideally, use another method to optimize exposure settings before shooting action sequences.

In Manual mode, it's often easier to vary the shutter speed or aperture yourself. If metered exposure is 1/125 at f/11, shooting extra frames at 1/60 sec. and 1/250 sec. gives the same result as a three-shot bracket with 1 Ev interval.

---

5) To cancel bracketing and return to normal shooting, press **?/o⟋** and rotate the main command dial until *OF* appears in the control panel and information display.

› Exposure lock

Many people find exposure lock a quick and intuitive way to fine-tune the camera's exposure setting. In Full Auto and Effects modes it's the only method available.

Exposure lock is useful where very dark or light areas (especially light sources) within the frame can overinfluence exposure. It lets you meter from a more average area, by pointing the camera in a different direction or stepping closer to the subject, then hold that exposure while reframing the shot you want.

Using Exposure lock
1) Aim the camera in a suitable direction, avoiding especially dark or light areas.

2) Half-press the shutter-release button to take a meter reading, then press and hold **AE-L/AF-L** to lock the exposure.

3) Keep pressing **AE-L/AF-L** as you reframe the image, then press the shutter-release button to shoot.

By default, **AE-L/AF-L** locks focus as well as exposure. This can be changed using Custom setting f2. You can also opt to lock exposure simply by keeping the shutter-release button half-pressed. Use Custom setting c1. And you can completely separate the functions of the **AE-L/AF-L** and shutter-release buttons by enabling back-button autofocus. This lets you use the shutter-release button for exposure lock without any limitations on autofocus.

Tip

Nikon advises against using exposure lock when you're using matrix metering, but there's no logical reason not to do so, if it helps.

EXPOSURE LOCK ⌄

Exposure lock can help keep the brightness of a subject consistent when it's moving against a variable background.
200mm, 1/500 sec., f/4, ISO 400.

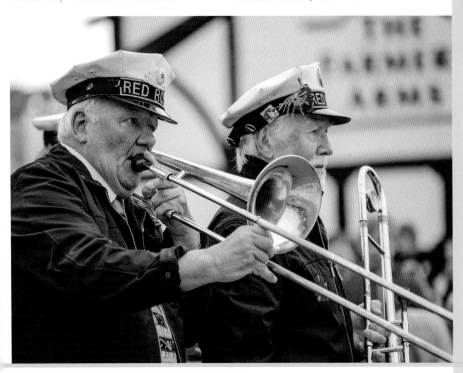

» WHITE BALANCE

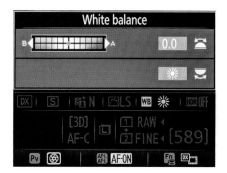

SETTING WHITE BALANCE IN THE INFORMATION DISPLAY ⌃

Light sources, natural and artificial, vary enormously in color. Our eyes and brain are very good—most of the time—at compensating for this and seeing people and objects in their "true" colors: we nearly always see grass as green, and so on. Digital cameras can also compensate for the varying colors of light. Used correctly, the D7200 can produce natural-looking colors under almost any conditions you'll ever encounter.

Automatic White Balance produces very good results most of the time, especially out of doors. For finer control, or for creative effect, a wide range of user-controlled settings are available, but only in **P**, **S**, **A**, or **M** modes.

When shooting RAW, the camera white balance (WB) setting is not crucial, as white balance can be adjusted in post-processing. However, it's still helpful to get it right as it does affect how images look on playback and review.

When shooting movies, where there's no RAW option, the right white balance setting can be vital, though using a Flat Picture Control does give you more room for maneuver.

Setting white balance

There are two ways to set white balance:

1) Hold down **?/o͞n** and rotate the main command dial until the required icon is displayed in the control panel. This is quicker, but method 2 offers extra options.

2) In the Photo Shooting menu, select **White balance**, then highlight and select the required setting. In most cases, a graphical display appears, with which you can fine-tune the setting (see page 68). Or just press ⓞⓚ to accept the standard value.

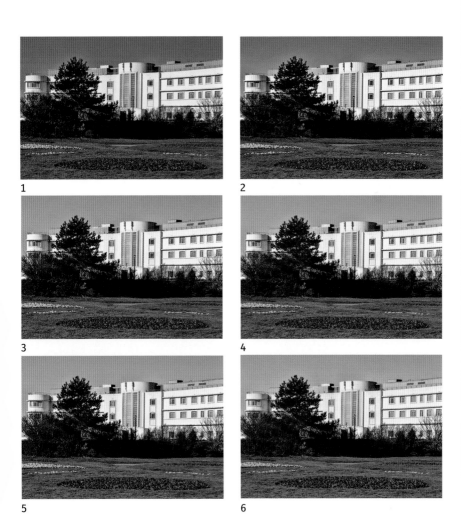

WHITE BALANCE COMPARISON ⌃
The effect of different white balance settings. Incandescent (1); Cool-white fluorescent (2); Direct sunlight (3); Flash (4); Cloudy (5); Shade (6).

The basic options offered by **?/Oπ** and the main command dial, or the top level in the Photo Shooting menu, are just the start.

Fine-tuning with the sub-command dial

For most of the standard WB settings, if you hold **?/Oπ** and turn the sub-command dial, you'll see a letter and number in the information display, alongside a graphical "spectrum". Turn the dial to the left to shift the image towards amber (**a1–a6**), to the right to shift towards blue (**b1–b6**).

Fine-tuning in the Photo Shooting menu

Auto has two sub-options: **Normal (AUTO1)**, which keeps colors correct as far as possible, and **Keep warm lighting colors (AUTO2)**, which does not fully correct warm hues such as those generated by incandescent lighting. This can work quite well for sunrise/sunset shots as well.

If you select **Incandescent**, **Direct sunlight**, **Flash**, **Cloudy**, or **Shade**, then press ▶, a graphical display appears and you can fine-tune the setting using the multi-selector. When done, press ⓞⓚ to accept the new value.

When you select **Fluorescent**, a submenu appears from which you can select the appropriate variety of fluorescent lamp. (The default is **4: Cool-**

white fluorescent.) If required, you can then press ▶ to do further fine-tuning, as above.

If you select **Fluorescent** with **?/Oπ** and the main command dial, the submenu is not available. The default will apply, unless you've previously changed the setting via the submenu.

ALL THAT GLITTERS ❮❮

Auto White Balance may not always give perfect results with strongly colored subjects—this Buddha looks a bit greener than it should.
112mm, 1/640 sec., f/5.6, ISO 200.

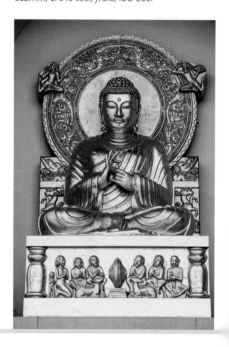

ICON	MENU OPTION		COLOR TEMP (°K)	DESCRIPTION
AUTO	AUTO	Normal	3500–8000	Camera sets white balance automatically, using information from imaging and metering sensors. Most accurate with Type G, D, or E lenses.
		Keep warm colors		
☀	Incandescent		3000	Use in incandescent (tungsten) lighting, e.g. traditional household bulbs.

Fluorescent: Sub-menu offers seven options:

ICON	MENU OPTION	COLOR TEMP (°K)	DESCRIPTION
	1) Sodium-vapor lamps	2700	Use in sodium-vapor lighting, often used in sports venues.
	2) Warm-white fluorescent	3000	Use in warm-white fluorescent lighting.
☼	3) White fluorescent	3700	Use in white fluorescent lighting.
	4) Cool-white fluorescent	4200	Use in cool-white fluorescent lighting.
	5) Day white fluorescent	5000	Use in daylight white fluorescent lighting.
	6) Daylight fluorescent	6500	Use in daylight fluorescent lighting.
	7) High temp mercury-vapor	7200	Use in high color temperature lighting, e.g. mercury vapor lamps.
☀	Direct sunlight	5200	Use for subjects in direct sunlight.
⚡	Flash	5400	Use with built-in flash or separate flashgun.
☁	Cloudy	6000	Use in daylight, under cloudy/overcast skies.
🏠	Shade	8000	Use on sunny days for subjects in shade.
K	Choose color temp.	2500–10000	Select color temperature from list of values.
PRE	Preset Manual	n/a	Derive white balance direct from subject or light source, or from an existing photo.

2 » COLOR SPACE

Color spaces define the range (or gamut) of colors which are recorded. To select the color space, use **Color space** in the Photo Shooting menu.

sRGB (the default setting) has a narrower gamut but images often appear brighter and more punchy. It's the standard color space on the Internet and in photo printing stores, for example, and is a safe choice for images that are likely to be used or printed straight off, with little or no post-processing.

Adobe RGB has a wider gamut and is commonly used in professional printing and reproduction. It's a better choice for images that are destined for professional applications or where significant post-processing is anticipated. However, images straight from the camera may look a little flat on most computers and web devices or if printed without full color management.

» IMAGE QUALITY

"Image quality" denotes the file type. The D7200 can record two kinds: NEF (RAW) and JPEG. JPEG files are processed in-camera to produce images that should be usable right away (e.g. for immediate printing), without post-processing on computer. However, JPEG processing discards much of the information originally captured by the sensor.

RAW files keep this data intact, leaving much greater scope for post-processing to achieve whatever pictorial qualities you desire. This requires suitable software (see Chapter 9). RAW or Camera RAW is a generic term for this kind of file; NEF is Nikon's specific RAW file format.

Because RAW files capture much more information than JPEGs, they produce larger file sizes. Inevitably, it takes longer to transfer them to the memory card. This limits the number of images you can shoot in a rapid continuous burst (see the Buffer, page 34).

RAW files can be recorded at either **12-bit** or **14-bit** depth. 14-bit files capture four times more color information than 12-bit, further limiting continuous shooting rate and burst numbers.

The D7200 can also simultaneously record two versions of the same image, one RAW and one JPEG.

The majority of Effects modes do not allow you to capture RAW files, because image processing is integral to these modes. When you use the Retouch menu, the end product is a JPEG image, as it is when you use HDR (high dynamic range).

› Choices

It's often assumed that RAW is used by "real photographers" and JPEG by casual snappers, but it's not that clear-cut. You can get great results shooting JPEG (especially at **Fine** quality setting). However, there's less room to "fix" images later. If you're serious about your images, shooting JPEG demands real consideration and care with exposure, white balance, Picture Control, and other settings.

› Setting image quality

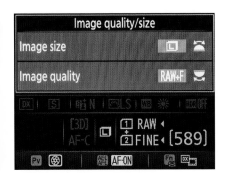

SETTING IMAGE QUALITY IN THE INFORMATION DISPLAY

There are two ways to set image quality:

1) Hold ⊕ and rotate the main command dial until the required setting is displayed in the control panel or information display.

2) In the Photo Shooting menu, select **Image quality**, then highlight the required setting and press ⊛.

To determine whether RAW files are recorded at 12-bit or 14-bit depth, select **NEF (RAW) recording** in the Photo Shooting menu, select **NEF (RAW)** bit depth, then select the desired option.

› JPEG quality options

JPEG images can be **Fine**, **Normal**, or **Basic**. The lower settings use higher levels of compression, which can produce visible "artefacts" when images are enlarged. Fine images (compression ratio approximately 1:4) should be suitable even for large prints. Normal (compression ratio approximately 1:8) should be suitable for modest-sized prints. Basic (compression ratio of approximately 1:16) is not recommended for printing but should be suitable for most online uses.

The default setting is Normal but I habitually use Fine (when not shooting RAW).

2 » IMAGE AREA AND IMAGE SIZE

There can be confusion between **Image area** and **Image size**. Image area refers to the portion of the sensor used to capture the image; Image size refers to the pixel count of the final image file.

› Image area

The D7200 normally captures images using the whole of its 23.5 x 15.6mm DX-format sensor (sometimes labeled 24 x 16). Alternatively, the **1.3x** crop setting captures images using a central 18 x 12mm area. This has several potential benefits. It allows more images to be recorded on a single memory card, and also allows a slightly higher maximum frame rate (7fps rather than 6fps). Perhaps more significantly, for action and wildlife shooters in particular, it increases the effective focal length of your lenses. It also means that the 51 focus points cover almost the entire image area, allowing continuous autofocus even on subjects near the edge of the frame.

Even with 1.3x crop in effect, NEF (RAW) and JPEG Large images still measure 4800 x 3200 pixels (15.4 megapixels). This is close to the 16.2mp of the D7200, and far more than you need for most purposes. Image area is normally selected using the item of that name in the Photo Shooting menu. If you switch Image area frequently, you can speed up the process by assigning the Fn, Preview, or *AE-L/AF-L* button to this task through Custom setting f2, f3, or f4 (select **Press + command dials**). See page 122.

You can also use 1.3x crop when shooting movie clips (page 174).

› Image size

For each image area, there are three options for image size. These only apply to JPEG images; RAW files are always recorded at Large size.

When using DX image area, **Medium** is roughly equivalent to a 14-megapixel camera, **Small** to a 6-megapixel camera. Even 1.3x cropped, Small images exceed the maximum resolution of almost all computer monitors and are well beyond the 2 megapixels (approximately) of an HD TV.

Image Area	Size (Large)	Size (Medium)	Size (Small)
DX (24 x 16)	6000 x 4000	4496 x 3000	2992 x 2000
1.3x (18 x 12)	4800 x 3200	3600 x 2400	2400 x 1600

Setting image size

There are two ways to set image size:

1) Hold 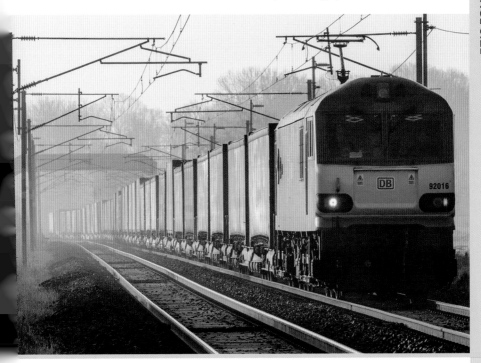 and rotate the sub-command dial until the required setting is shown in the information display.

2) In the Photo Shooting menu, select **Image size**, then highlight and select the required setting.

FOCUS OPTIONS ⌄

1.3x crop allows you to maintain continuous AF, even with subjects near the edge of the frame. *200mm, 1/640 sec., f/8, ISO 400.*

2 » FOCUSING

There are multiple focus-related options, but they all boil down to *where* and *how*.

Where the camera focuses is determined by the AF-area modes. These aim to ensure that the camera focuses on the desired subject, or sometimes—especially in close-up photography—the right part of the subject.

How the camera focuses is determined by the focus modes. These determine whether the camera automatically refocuses if the subject moves, or only when you tell it to.

This basic distinction applies whether you're using the viewfinder, in Live View, or shooting movies. However, the detailed options are different for Live View and movies. This section only deals with viewfinder-based focusing.

Having focused at a certain distance, depth of field then determines how much of the rest of the image will also be sharp.

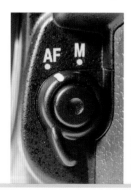

FOCUS
SELECTOR   «
SWITCH

› Focus modes

To switch between manual focus and autofocus use the selector switch on the left front of the camera. To choose the AF mode, press ⊙, in the center of this switch, and rotate the main command dial; as you do this, the settings appear in all the displays.

In some Effects modes, options are limited. Manual focus can always be selected, but the only autofocus option is **AF-A**.

AF-A Auto-servo AF

AF-A means that the camera automatically switches between single-servo AF and continuous-servo AF (see below).

AF-S Single-servo AF

The camera focuses when the shutter release is pressed halfway. Focus remains locked on this point while you maintain half-pressure. The camera will not take a picture unless focus has been acquired (**focus priority**). This mode is recommended for accurate focusing on static subjects.

AF-C Continuous-servo AF

In this mode, suitable for moving subjects, the camera continues to seek focus as long as you maintain half-pressure on the

Tip

The focus priority/release priority settings can be changed using Custom settings a1 and a2.

shutter release: if the subject moves, the camera will refocus. The camera can take a picture even if focus has not been acquired (**release priority**).

› Manual focus

With sophisticated autofocus available, manual focus might appear redundant, but many photographers like to retain control. You might also want to use an old manual focus lens (take care—see page 184). AF may also struggle with certain subjects and in extremely low light.

Manual focusing requires little description: set the focus selector to **M** (do the same with the A/M switch on the lens, if there is one). Turn the focusing ring on the lens to bring the subject into focus.

› Focus confirmation

When focusing manually, you can still exploit the camera's autofocus sensor.

Select an appropriate focus area, as if you were using autofocus. Arrows at bottom left of the viewfinder show whether focus in that area is in front of or behind the subject. When the subject is in focus a dot appears in place of the arrows.

› AF-area modes

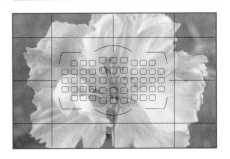

VIEWFINDER ⌃
The viewfinder displays the available focus areas as well as an in-focus indicator at the left of the menu bar.

The D7200 has 51 focus points (or focus areas), covering an area indicated by a faint outline in the viewfinder. When you half-press the shutter release, the currently active focus point(s) illuminate briefly in red. (Illumination can be switched off using Custom setting a4.)

AF-area modes determine which of these focus point(s) the camera will use to focus on the subject.

To choose AF-area mode, press ⦿ and rotate the sub-command dial. The viewfinder, control panel, and information display show the selected mode.

Auto-area AF ▣

This mode makes focus point selection fully automatic, effectively letting the camera decide what the subject is. With Type G, D, or E lenses, the camera employs face-detection technology, and if a face is detected will prioritize it for focusing.

Single-area AF [⸤⸥]

You select the focus area, using the multi-selector to move through the 51 focus points. The chosen focus point is illuminated in the viewfinder. This mode suits relatively static subjects, and allies naturally with **AF-S** autofocus mode.

Dynamic-area AF [⸤ː⸥]

This mode is more complicated, as it has several sub-modes. These can only be selected when the **AF** mode is **AF-A** or **AF-C**. You still select the initial focus point, as in Single-area AF, but if the subject moves, the camera will employ other focus points to try and maintain focus on the chosen subject.

The sub-mode options determine the number of focus points that will be employed for this: 9, 21, or the full 51 points.

The final option is **[3D]** 3D tracking, which uses additional information, including subject colors, to track subjects that may be moving erratically.

Focus point selection

1) Ensure the camera is set to Single-point AF or Dynamic-area AF. Check the focus selector lock, around the multi-selector, is unlocked (align the white dots).

2) Using the multi-selector, move the active focus point to the desired position.

3) Half-press the shutter-release button to focus at the desired point; press fully to take the shot.

Tip

Pressing ⊛ jumps directly to the central focus point (unless you change the options in Custom setting f1). Focus point wrap-around (Custom setting a6) lets you "jump" directly from farthest left points to farthest right, or vice versa.

SHIFTING FOCUS POINTS »
Shifting the focus point changes the emphasis.
150mm, 1/1000 sec., f/5.6, ISO 100.

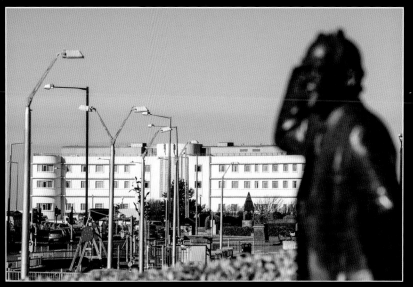

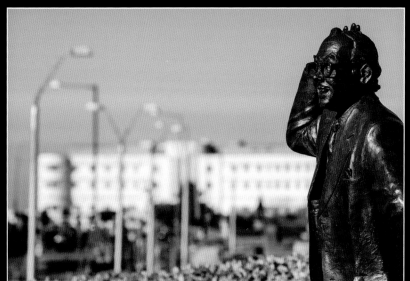

› Focus lock

The D7200's focus points cover a wide area but do not reach the edges of the frame. If they don't cover the subject, you can use focus lock. It's similar in principle to exposure lock. You shift the camera until the subject is within the area covered by the focus points, then select a focus point and focus on the subject in the normal way.

You then reframe the image to get the subject in the right place while keeping focus locked. In **AF-S** mode, lock focus by keeping half-pressure on the shutter-release button, or by holding down **AE-L/AF-L**. In **AF-C**, only **AE-L/AF-L** can be used. Maintain pressure on the button to keep focus locked for further shots.

F FOR FANTASTIC ⌄
I focused on the "F" of "Fantastic".
185mm, 1/500 sec., f/4, ISO 100.

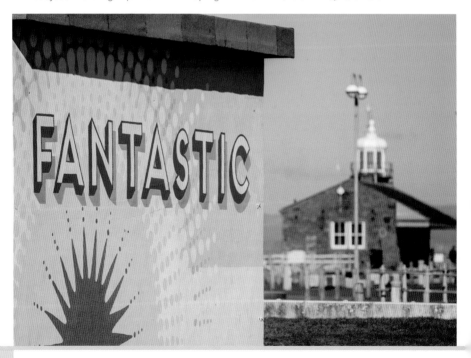

Focus lock can also be useful in low light, as the 15 central AF points are more sensitive. You can focus using one of these, lock, and then reframe to place the subject off-center.

› AF-assist illuminator

A small lamp is available to help the camera focus in dim light. It illuminates automatically when required, provided (a) the focus mode is **AF-A** or **AF-S**, and (b) the central focus point is selected or Auto-area **AF** is engaged. Obviously, its range is limited. It can be turned off using Custom setting a9, and is always off in some Scene modes.

THE AF-ASSIST ILLUMINATOR ⊻

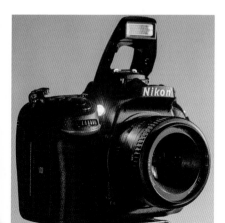

› Back-button autofocus

At standard settings, holding **AE-L/AF-L** locks both exposure and focus. You can use custom setting f4 to change its behavior to lock focus only, or exposure only. And there's another option: **AF-ON only**.

When you choose this option, the shutter-release button no longer controls autofocus; you can initiate **AF** only by pressing **AE-L/AF-L**. Many pros use this approach, often called "back-button AF". The logic is that you can switch seamlessly between **AF-C** and **AF-S**, without any pause in shooting. First, set the camera to **AF-C**. Now, if you press **AE-L/AF-L**, focus, and release it, the camera does not refocus when you press the shutter-release button. It only does so when you press **AE-L/AF-L** again. This effectively duplicates **AF-S**, even though the camera is set to **AF-C.** However, if you maintain pressure on **AE-L/AF-L**, AF-C operates normally.

Back-button **AF** also means that you can use the shutter-release button for exposure lock, simply by keeping it half-pressed. It may take a little acclimatization, but soon becomes second nature, with the right thumb in charge of focus and the index finger in charge of exposure.

2 » DEPTH OF FIELD

We noted on page 52 that aperture is one of the key factors governing depth of field. However, depth of field is a complex business and other key factors are the focal length of the lens and the distance to the subject.

Sometimes, shallow depth of field is exactly what you want, as it makes the subject stand out against a soft background. For other images you may want to try and have everything sharp from front to back: this is traditional (but not compulsory!) in landscape photography.

With long lenses and/or nearby subjects, depth of field may remain shallow even at small apertures. This is very evident in macro photography (see Chapter 5). It's equally true that, with wide-angle lenses, unless the subject is very close, it's not easy to get the sort of shallow depth of field that makes it really stand out from the background.

› Depth of field preview

When you look through the viewfinder, the lens is set at its widest aperture; if a smaller

CLOSE FOCUSING ⌄
At close range, especially in macro shooting, depth of field is inescapably narrow.
100mm macro, 1/100 sec., f/11, ISO 100, beanbag.

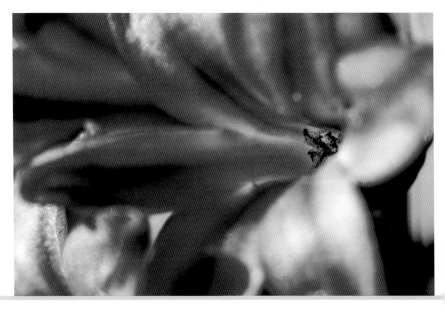

aperture is selected, the lens stops down at the moment the picture is actually taken. As a result, the viewfinder image can have much less depth of field than the final shot. The depth of field preview (Pv) button stops the lens down to the selected aperture. However, this darkens the image and assessing sharpness isn't always easy.

Fortunately, there are alternatives. One is by using Live View. When you enter Live View, the camera stops down to the currently set aperture. However, it doesn't immediately readjust if you change the aperture setting while in Live View. It will only reset the aperture when you take a

picture, or if you exit and resume Live View. You can also get a sense of depth of field by taking a test shot and viewing it on screen. Both Live View and image review allow you to zoom in for a closer look. This can be a slow process but does give you a very good idea of what is (or isn't) going to appear sharp in the final image.

BRING ME SUNSHINE ⌄
I wanted the background soft, but not so soft that it became unrecognizable; a middling aperture worked well for this.
155mm, 1/400 sec., f/7.1, ISO 100, tripod.

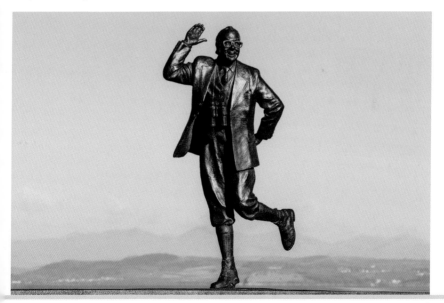

2 » IMAGE ENHANCEMENT

The D7200 offers two main kinds of in-camera image adjustment or enhancement. First, certain settings can be applied before shooting an image; these are covered in this section. Second, you can create retouched copies of existing images on the memory card; this is done via the Retouch menu (see page 134).

Many of the controls that we've already considered—like aperture, shutter speed, ISO, and white balance—have obvious and direct effects in the final image. In **P**, **S**, **A**, or **M** modes, you can access other settings affecting the qualities of the image, notably Nikon Picture Controls and Active D-Lighting.

These affect how the camera processes JPEG images. When shooting RAW, they have no effect on the basic raw data. However, they do affect the appearance of review/playback images on the monitor, even when the base image is RAW.

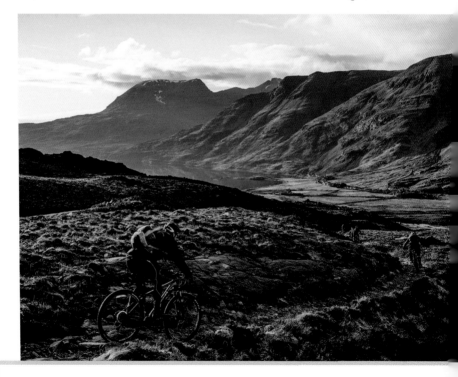

› Active D-Lighting

Active D-Lighting enhances the D7200's ability to cope with scenes that show a wide range of brightness (dynamic range). Essentially, it reduces overall exposure to capture more highlight detail. Mid-tones and shadows are then lightened as the camera processes the image. Don't confuse it with the similarly-named D-Lighting, which is a Retouch menu option.

Access Active D-Lighting from the Photo Shooting menu, or by pressing **▸🖪▸** to reveal the Quick settings screen. Select **Off**, **Low**, **Normal**, **High**, **Extra high**, or **Auto** to determine the strength of the effect, then press ㋛. This setting applies to all images until you reset Active D-Lighting.

> ### *Tip*
>
> *Because Active D-Lighting alters the overall exposure, it's advisable to turn it off when shooting RAW.*

FOLLOWING THE TRAIL «
Active D-Lighting works with moving subjects, which can give odd results with HDR.
45mm, 1/320sec., f/8, ISO 200.

› Nikon Picture Controls

Picture Controls influence the way JPEG files are processed by the camera. They also affect the preview image associated with each RAW file, on which Histogram and Highlights displays are based. In addition, they affect the appearance of the Live View preview image.

Picture Controls are predetermined in Auto, Scene, and Effects modes, but in **P**, **S**, **A**, or **M** modes you have a free hand to choose and fine-tune them. In all modes the current Picture Control is indicated in the information display.

You can select Picture Controls from the Photo Shooting menu, or by pressing **▸🖪▸** to reveal the Quick settings screen.

The D7200 has seven pre-loaded Picture Controls: **Standard**, **Neutral**, **Vivid**, **Monochrome**, **Portrait**, **Landscape**, and **Flat**. These are mostly fairly self-explanatory. Portrait, for example, uses moderate settings for contrast, sharpening, and saturation, aiming to deliver natural colors and flattering skin tones. The Flat Picture Control deserves additional explanation (see page 85).

Each has preset values for **Sharpening**, **Clarity**, **Contrast**, and **Brightness**. For color images, there are also settings for **Saturation** and **Hue**; Monochrome has **Filter effects** and **Toning** instead. You can fine-tune these values within each Picture Control. You can also create and save your own custom Picture Controls.

Modifying Picture Controls

From the Photo Shooting menu or quick settings screen, select **Set Picture Control**, highlight the required Picture Control, then press ▶. Select **Quick Adjust** or one of the specific parameters. Use ▶ or ◀ to change the values. When all parameters are as required, press ⊛. Modified values are retained until you modify that Picture Control again.

Custom Picture Controls

You can create up to nine additional Picture Controls in-camera. Select **Manage Picture Control** from the Photo Shooting menu. Select **Save/edit** and press ▶. Highlight an existing Picture Control and press ▶ again. Edit the Picture Control as described under Modifying Picture Controls. When satisfied, press ⊛.

By default, the new version takes its name from the existing Picture Control on

FLOWER POWER ≫
Picture Controls: Vivid (left side) and Flat (right).
200mm, 1/160 sec., f/8, ISO 100, tripod

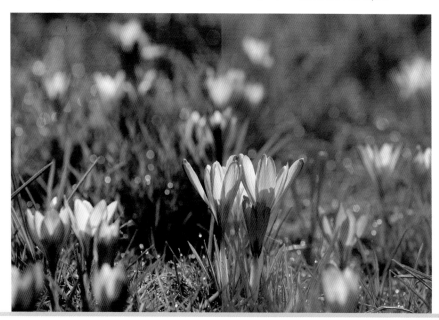

which it is based, plus a two-digit number (e.g. VIVID-02). You can give it a new name (up to 19 characters long) using the multi-selector to enter text. (For more on text entry see page 107.) Finally, press (OK) to store the new Picture Control.

Nikon's Picture Control Utility 2 (free download on Mac and PC) lets you make even more refined adjustments to existing or new Picture Controls.

Flat Picture Control

The Flat Picture Control produces images which appear very subdued, with low contrast and saturation and no in-camera sharpening. It is aimed mainly at movie-makers who intend to work on the color, contrast, and so on, of their footage in post-production ("grading"). It's designed to give the most room for later adjustments, thereby allowing movie shooters some of the flexibility and control that stills photographers gain by shooting RAW.

It can have value for stills photographers too, at least when shooting RAW. As mentioned above, the Histogram and Highlights displays are based on the JPEG preview embedded with each RAW file. As such, they will give a more accurate guide to the potential of the RAW file when you use a Flat Picture Control. However, the "dull" preview image may be a poor indication of the appearance of the final,

post-processed, RAW file, so you need to be prepared to rely mainly on the Histogram and Highlights displays.

› HDR (high dynamic range) images

"Contrast", "dynamic range", "tonal range": all refer to the range of brightness between the brightest and darkest areas of a scene. Our eyes adjust continuously, allowing us to see detail in both bright areas and deep shade. By comparison, even the best cameras can fall short, losing detail ("clipping") in shadows, highlights, or even both.

Possible remedies include shooting RAW, using Active D-Lighting for JPEG images, or fill-in flash. Even so, sometimes it's impossible to capture the entire brightness range of a scene in a single exposure. The histogram and highlights displays help identify such cases.

One solution is to shoot several exposures and then combine the results. The D7200 can automate this, creating a high dynamic range JPEG by merging two separate shots, with one exposure biased towards the shadows and one towards the highlights. HDR can be combined with Active D-Lighting for even greater range.

Because HDR merges two exposures, it can give odd results with moving subjects.

2

Shooting an HDR image

1) From the Photo Shooting menu, select **HDR (high dynamic range)**. It is unavailable if **Image quality** is set to RAW. Select **HDR mode** and press ▶.

2) Select **On (series)** to take a series of HDR images. Select **On (single photo)** to take just one. An HDR icon appears in the control panel.

3) Choose **HDR strength** (essentially the difference in exposure between the two source images). **Auto** allows the camera to determine this automatically, or you can select **Low**, **Normal**, **High**, or **Extra High**.

4) Shoot as normal. The camera will automatically shoot two images in quick succession. It then takes a few moments to combine them and display the results. During this time *Job* flashes in the viewfinder and you can't take further shots.

5) If you selected **On (series)** at step 2, HDR shooting continues until you visit the menu again to cancel it. If you selected **On (single photo)**, it's automatically canceled.

Tip

You can take HDR photography much further by bracketing exposures and using HDR software on the computer. I've often used the LR/Enfuse plugin for Adobe Lightroom, but the latest version (Lightroom CC) has native HDR merge ability. I also merge images manually using Photoshop's Layer Masks.

WRECKAGE »
An in-camera HDR image (HDR strength High) and two (simulated) source frames (insets). *12mm, "source" images: 1/125 and 1/30 sec., f/11, ISO 100, tripod.*

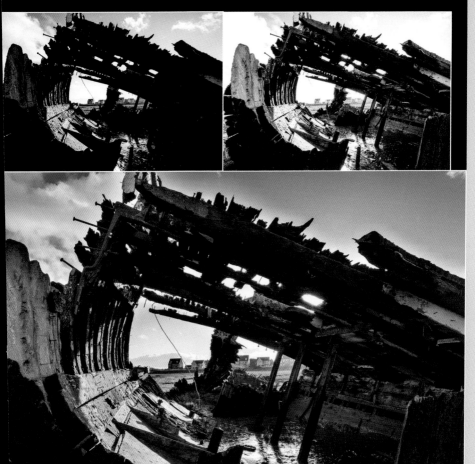

The mode dial's U1 and U2 positions allow instant access to predetermined combinations of camera settings. You can take a "snapshot" of how the camera is set up at a particular moment, including everything from exposure mode to menu settings. If you use Manual, the camera will even recall shutter speed and aperture. You can then return it to that state at any time simply by turning the mode dial to U1 or U2.

One application for User settings is when the camera is shared between two people. For example, you may like full

SPEED CYCLE ☰
User settings let you store and recall settings suitable for a specific venue.
100mm, 1/1000 sec., f/2.8, ISO 1600.

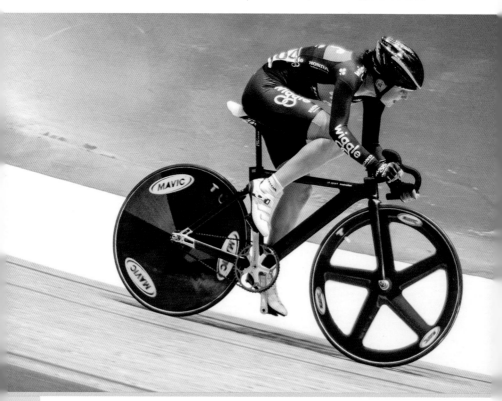

manual control, but sometimes hand the camera to a partner or child who likes things much simpler. U1 could be your setting, with the camera in Manual mode, and preferred values for settings like white balance and **AF** mode already dialed in. U2 could link to a preferred Scene mode for the secondary user. (There's no point in linking to ⚙ or ⚡ as these are directly accessible from the mode dial anyway.)

Another application is if you regularly shoot under repeatable conditions or at a particular location, e.g. shooting sports in a particular stadium or weddings at a certain venue. You can establish ISO, white balance, and all the other settings which produce the best results, then save them to User settings. On your next visit you can restore all of these settings with a single turn of the mode dial.

Whenever you turn the dial to U1 or U2, the recorded combination of settings is just a starting point; you can adjust all settings as normal. You can subsequently turn the dial to **P**, **S**, **A**, or **M** without losing any of the other settings. However if you switch to Auto, Scene, or Effects modes, their standard settings kick in.

To store User settings

1) Ensure the camera is set up, in all respects, as you require. Even in Auto or Scene modes, many options remain open. In **P**, **S**, **A**, or **M** mode you can work through an even wider range of settings.

2) Go to **Save user settings** in the Setup menu and press ▶.

3) Highlight **U1** or **U2** and press ▶.

4) Highlight **Save settings** and press ⓞⓚ.

To reset User settings

To create a new set of User settings for either dial position, replacing an earlier set, simply repeat the procedure above. Don't use **Reset user settings** in the Setup menu; this will revert all settings at U1 or U2 to the camera's default values (e.g. exposure mode=Auto, Image quality=JPEG Normal, and so on).

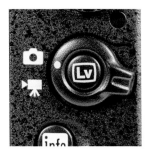

**LIVE VIEW «
ACTIVATION
SWITCH**

DSLRs like the D7200 are designed around the viewfinder. This still has many advantages for the majority of picture-taking. It's more intuitive and offers a sense of direct connection with the subject. There's much less risk of camera shake, and viewfinder-based autofocus is faster.

However, to fully realize the high image quality of today's cameras, discerning shooters use tripods regularly; this dilutes the ergonomic advantages of the viewfinder. Also, Live View focusing, though much slower than viewfinder-based AF, is extremely accurate. Live View may sometimes facilitate shooting from awkward positions where you can't use the viewfinder. Live View gives you an alternative depth of field preview and the Live View screen image reflects the current Picture Control (including Monochrome).

Live View is also the starting point for shooting movies (Chapter 6), so familiarity with Live View is helpful here.

> Using Live View

Check the **Lv** switch on the rear of the camera is set to the ◘ still photography position. Press its center button to activate Live View. The mirror flips up, the viewfinder blacks out, and the monitor displays a continuous live image. Press the release button fully to take a picture, as when shooting normally. In continuous release modes the mirror stays up between shots, so the monitor remains blank, making it hard to follow moving subjects. To exit Live View press the center button again.

> Live View display options

A range of shooting information is displayed at top and bottom of the screen, partly overlaying the image. Pressing **info** changes this display, cycling through a series of screens (see the table opposite).

LIVE VIEW VIRTUAL HORIZON INDICATOR ☆

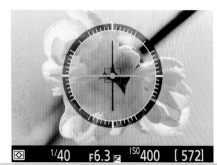

LIVE VIEW OPTIONS	DETAILS
Show detailed photo indicators (default)	Information bars superimposed at top and bottom of screen.
Hide all indicators	Top information bar disappears, key shooting information still shown at bottom.
Framing grid	Grid lines appear, useful for critical framing.
Virtual horizon	Displays a horizon indicator on the monitor to assist in leveling the camera.

› Live View quick settings

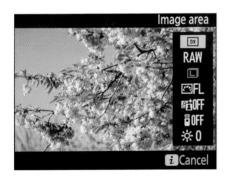

LIVE VIEW QUICK SETTINGS

Key settings (see below) can be quickly adjusted in Live View. Press ◀❚▶ to reveal these items at the right side of the screen. Scroll up or down using ▲ / ▼; press ▶ or ⊛ to access the highlighted item.

Live View quick settings
Image area—see page 72.
Image quality—see page 70.
Image size—see page 72.
Set Picture Control—see page 83.
Active D-Lighting—see page 83.
Remote control mode (ML-L3)—see page 29.

Monitor brightness—Adjust screen brightness with ▲ / ▼. This only affects the Live View screen image, not the exposure level of actual images.

2

› Focusing in Live View

Focusing in Live View operates differently from normal shooting; because the mirror is locked up, the usual focusing sensor is unavailable. Instead, the camera reads focus information directly from the main image sensor. This is slower than normal AF operation—often conspicuously so—but very accurate. You can also zoom in the view, which helps in placing the focus point precisely where you want it. This aids manual focusing too.

Live View has its own set of autofocus options, with two AF modes and four AF-area modes. Select these when Live View is active. Hold ⊙ and use the main

FOCUSING IN LIVE VIEW ⌄

The focus area (a red rectangle, which turns green when focus is acquired) can be positioned anywhere on screen, and the view can be zoomed for greater precision.

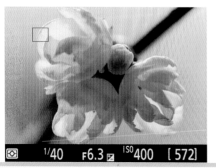

command dial to select AF mode. Use ⊙ and the sub-command dial to select the AF-area mode.

Live View AF modes

The AF-mode options are **Single-servo AF (AF-S)** and **Full-time servo AF (AF-F)**.

AF-S corresponds to AF-S in normal shooting: the camera focuses when the shutter release is pressed halfway, and focus remains locked as long as the shutter release remains depressed.

AF-F corresponds roughly to AF-C in normal shooting, but responds differently to the shutter-release button (or **AE-L/AF-L** if you are using back-button AF). The camera seeks focus as long as Live View remains active. When you half-press the button, focus locks, and remains locked until you release the button, or take a shot.

Live View AF-area mode

There are four Live View AF-area modes (see table opposite). They are different from those used in normal shooting, but perform the same basic function, i.e. determining how the focus point is selected. Again, selection is through the active information display—except in 🏛️, ⚘, and 🏃, where AF-area mode is predetermined.

AF-AREA MODE	DESCRIPTION
🔘 Face priority	Uses face detection to identify people. Yellow border appears outlining faces. If multiple subjects are detected the camera focuses on the closest. Fixed in 📷ᴬᵁᵀᴼ, ⊛; default in most Scene modes.
▢ Wide-area	Camera analyzes focus information from area (shown by red rectangle) approximately ⅛ width/height of the frame. Fixed in 👤; default in 🏃, 🏢, 🐾, and most Effects modes.
▢ Normal area	Camera analyzes focus information from a much smaller area, shown by red rectangle. Useful for precise focusing on small subjects. Default in 🌷 and 🍴.
⊕ Subject tracking	Camera follows selected subject as it moves within the frame. Not available in 🏔, 🌃, ⊕, and 🧸.

Using Live View AF
▢ Wide-area AF and ▢ Normal area AF
In both these modes, the focus point (outlined in red) can be moved anywhere on the screen, using the multi-selector. Press ⊕ to zoom in on the current focus point. This gives ultra-precise focus control, ideal for macro photography, especially when shooting on a tripod. Having placed the focus point, focus by half-pressing the shutter-release button. The red rectangle turns green when focus is achieved.

PETAL PRECISION ⌄
Normal area AF is the best choice for precision and accuracy.
100mm macro, 1/60 sec., f/11, ISO 200, tripod.

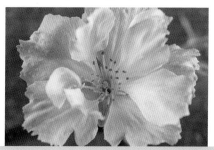

2

👁 Face-priority AF

In this mode, the camera automatically detects up to 35 faces and selects the closest, outlining it with a double yellow border. You can override it to focus on a different person by shifting the focus point with the multi-selector.

👁 Subject tracking

When you select Subject tracking, a white rectangle appears on the screen. Align this with the desired subject using the multi-selector, then press ⓞⓚ. The camera "memorizes" the subject and the rectangle turns yellow. It will now track the subject as it moves, and can even (sometimes) reacquire the subject if it briefly leaves the frame. To focus, press the shutter-release button halfway; the target rectangle blinks green while focusing, and then becomes solid green. If the camera fails to focus it blinks red instead. To restart (i.e. to pick a new target), press ⓞⓚ again.

Warning!

Subject tracking sounds great in theory, but it's far too slow for rapidly moving subjects. Viewfinder shooting is much more effective for real action photography.

Manual focus

Manual focus is engaged as in normal shooting. The great advantage of Live View for manual focusing is that you can zoom in by pressing ⊕: the zoom centers on the current focus point. For static subjects, this is the most precise form of focusing available. It is my usual choice for macro shooting in particular.

› Live View white balance

You can change white balance settings quickly in Live View: hold **?/⊶** and rotate the main command dial; the selected setting is highlighted in yellow at the top of the screen, and the preview image changes to reflect the new setting. You can fine-tune the value with the sub-command dial.

› Aperture in Live View

Unlike viewfinder photography, where the aperture remains wide open until the shot is taken, in Live View the lens is stopped down. This effectively offers a continuous depth of field preview. However, if you change the aperture setting, it doesn't actually update until you exit and re-enter Live View (or take a photo).

» PLAYBACK

The D7200's high-resolution LCD screen makes image playback both pleasurable and highly informative. It gives a good indication of how images will look on a computer screen or mobile device, if not in print.

To display the most recent image, press ▶ ; if **Image Review** is **On**, images are also displayed automatically after shooting. In continuous release modes, Image review begins after the last image in a burst is captured; images appear in sequence.

› Playback zoom

To assess sharpness, or for other critical viewing, you can zoom in on a section of an image.

1) Press 🔍 (up to 10 times) to zoom the currently selected image. A small navigation window appears briefly, with a yellow outline indicating the visible area.

2) Use the multi-selector to view other areas of the image.

3) Rotate the command dial to see other images at the same magnification.

4) To return to full-frame viewing, press 🆗 .

10 presses on 🔍 gives 200% magnification. This shows a pixelated image of debatable value; even the best images no longer look properly sharp! Eight presses gives 100% magnification. The bar at the bottom of the navigation window turns green at this zoom level.

You can program 🆗 to jump straight to a desired magnification level (**50%**, **100%**, or **200%**). Use Custom setting f1> **Playback mode> Zoom on/off**.

> **Note:**
> To conserve the battery, the monitor turns off after a period of inactivity. The default is 10 seconds, but intervals from 4 sec. to 10 min. can be set using Custom setting c4.

› Viewing photo information

The D7200 records masses of information (metadata) about each image taken, and this can also be viewed on playback, using ▲ / ▼ to scroll through up to nine pages of information (see table overleaf).

To determine which pages are visible, visit **Playback display options** in the Playback menu. Enable/disable options with ▶ ; press 🆗 to confirm and exit.

› Viewing other images

To view other images on the memory card, use ▶ to view images in the order of capture, ◀ to view in reverse order ("go back in time").

Viewing images as thumbnails

From most screens (not RGB histogram or highlights), press ♉☷ to display four images; repeat to see 9 or 72 images.

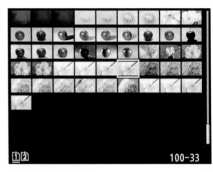

100-33

THUMBNAIL VIEW   ⌃

PLAYBACK PAGES	SELECTION	DETAILS
Basic photo info	Always available	Displays large image, basic file info displayed at bottom of screen.
RGB histogram	Enable from Playback menu	See page 98.
Highlights	Enable from Playback menu	See page 99.
Overview	Enable from Playback menu	Displays small image, simplified histogram, summary information. Focus point used can also be shown: select using **Playback display options>Focus point**.
Shooting data (three or four pages)	Enable from Playback menu	Pages 1–3 are always available. Page 4 only appears when Copyright Information is recorded.
None (image only)	Enable from Playback menu	Displays large image with no other data.
Location data	Only appears when GPS location data was recorded during shooting	

Press ⊕ to see fewer. The currently selected image is outlined in yellow.

Memory card selection

A small icon at bottom left on the Basic photo info or Thumbnail screens shows which memory card is currently being used for playback. To switch between card slots, press ⟨🔁⟩, select **Playback slot and folder**, highlight the desired slot and press ⊛.

Calendar View

Calendar View displays images grouped by the date on which they were taken. With 72 images displayed, press ⊖❑❑ again to reach the first calendar page (date view). The most recent date is highlighted, and pictures from that date appear in a strip on the right (the thumbnail list). Use the multi-selector to select other dates. Press ⊖❑❑ again to enter the thumbnail list so you can scroll through

pictures from the selected date; press ⊕ for a larger preview of the selected image.

Deleting images

To delete the current image, or the selected image in thumbnail view, press 🗑. A confirmation dialog appears. To proceed, press 🗑 again; to cancel, press ▶ .

In Calendar View you can also delete all images taken on a selected date. Highlight that date in Date View, then press 🗑; when the confirmation dialog appears press 🗑 again to delete or ▶ to cancel.

Protecting images

To protect the current image, press ?/⟨🔑⟩ . To remove protection, press again. Protected images can't be deleted as above, but will be deleted when the memory card is formatted.

MEMORY CARD SLOT SELECTION　　　❯❯

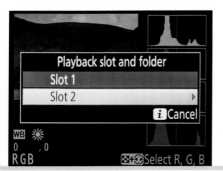

CALENDAR VIEW　　　❯❯

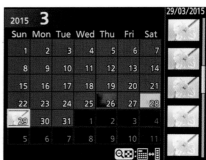

2

› Histogram displays

The histogram is a kind of graph showing the distribution of dark and light tones in an image. For assessing whether images are correctly exposed it's much more objective than examining the playback image itself—especially in bright conditions, when it's hard to see the screen image clearly.

The overview page shows a single histogram; checking **RGB histogram** under **Playback display options** in the Playback menu gives access to a display showing individual histograms for the three color channels (red, green, and blue). The histogram display is a core feature of image playback and usually the page I view first.

For more on this, see Chapter 3.

When shooting RAW, the Histogram (and Highlights) displays are based on the JPEG preview embedded with each RAW file. They are not, therefore, a foolproof guide to the potential for recovering highlight or shadow detail in that RAW file. This is particularly true when using "punchy" Picture Controls such as Vivid or Landscape, where JPEG processing discards more of the RAW data. Setting a Flat Picture Control makes the preview image look much duller, but means that histogram (and highlights) displays give a much better indication of the full potential of the RAW file.

RGB HISTOGRAM DISPLAY   ❯❯

This histogram shows a good spread of tones. Not surprisingly, there's more "volume" in the red channel and there is also a tiny spike at the right end in this channel; this indicates highlight clipping, obviously in the bright spot on the apple.

RGB HISTOGRAM DISPLAY   ❯❯

A typical "landscape histogram", with obvious twin peaks. The larger left-hand peak represents largely low to middle tones in the land while the smaller one represents the brighter tones of the sky.

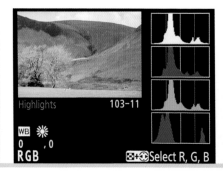

› Highlights display

The D7200 can also display a flashing warning for areas of the image with "clipped" highlights, i.e. completely white areas with no detail recorded. This is another useful and objective method for checking exposure.

HIGHLIGHTS DISPLAY ⌄ »
This image is taken from Adobe Lightroom, and the highlights are shown in red (right); in the camera display, these areas would flash black, but this doesn't show well on a printed page. *70mm, 1/500 sec., f/8 , ISO 200.*

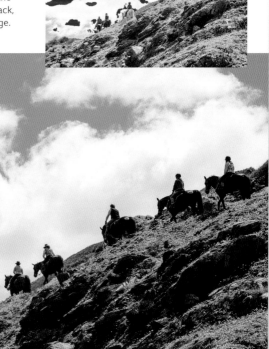

3 MENUS

The options in the preceding chapter are just the beginning. The menus offer many more ways to customize the D7200 to suit your needs. There are six main menus: **Playback, Shooting, Custom Setting, Setup, Retouch,** and **My Menu/Recent Settings.**

The **Playback menu** covers functions related to playback, including viewing and deleting images. The **Photo Shooting menu** is used to control shooting settings, such as ISO, white balance, or Active D-Lighting, though many of these, can be accessed—often more easily—by other means. The **Movie Shooting menu** serves a similar role for movie options. The **Custom Setting menu** lets you fine-tune and personalize many aspects of the camera's operation. The **Setup menu** governs functions ranging from LCD brightness to language and time settings. The **Retouch menu** lets you create modified copies of images you've already taken. Finally, **My Menu** is a handy place to store items from the other menus that you find yourself using regularly. Alternatively, it can become a **Recent Settings menu**.

Navigating the menus

1) To display the main menu screen, press **MENU**.

2) Scroll up or down to highlight individual menus. To enter the desired menu, press ▶.

3) Scroll up or down to highlight specific menu items. To select an item, press ▶. In most cases this will take you to a further set of options.

4) Scroll up or down to the desired setting. To select, press ▶ or ⊛. In some cases you need to scroll up to **Done** and press ⊛ to make changes effective.

LOOKING AT EWE »
Menus give access to an enormous range of options—including monochrome images.
110mm, 1/200 sec., f/11, ISO 250.

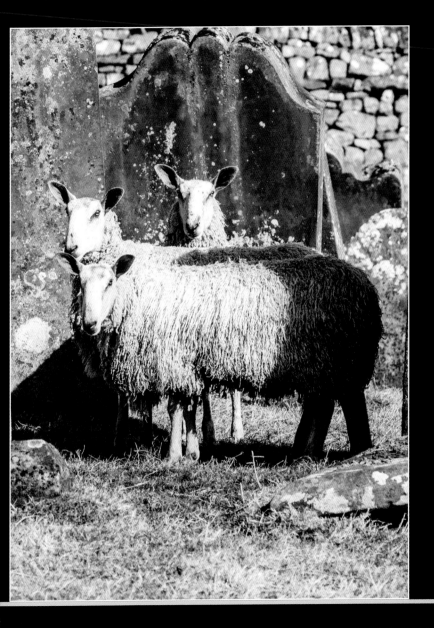

3

» PLAYBACK MENU

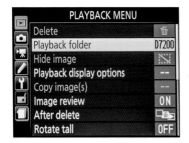

The Playback menu contains 10 items which affect how images are viewed, stored, shared, deleted, and printed. Most of these are only accessible when a memory card—with image(s)—is present in the camera.

› Delete

This function allows images stored on the memory card to be deleted, either singly or in batches. Headings within the menu are **Selected**, **Date**, or **ALL**.

If you choose Selected, images in the active playback folder or folders (see below) are displayed as thumbnails. Use the multi-selector to scroll through them. Press

Tip

Individual images can also be deleted from the normal playback screen, and this is usually more convenient (see page 97).

⊕ to view the highlighted image full-screen. Press ⊖▦ to mark the highlighted shot for deletion; it's tagged with 🗑. If you change your mind, highlight a tagged image and press ⊖▦ again to remove the tag.

Repeat this procedure to select further images. Press ⑥ to see a confirmation screen. Select **YES** and press ⑥ to delete the selected image(s); to exit without deleting any images, select **NO**.

If you choose **Date**, you'll see a list of dates on which images on the memory card were taken. Use the multi-selector to scroll through the list. Press ▶ to mark the highlighted date for deletion. It will be checked in the list. If you change your mind, highlight the date and press ▶ again to remove the tag.

Repeat this procedure to select further dates. Press ⑥ to see a confirmation screen. Select **YES** and press ⑥ to delete all image(s) taken on the selected date(s).

› Playback folder

By default, the playback screen will only display images created on the D7200: if a memory card is inserted which contains images from a different model of camera (even another Nikon DSLR) they will not be visible. This can be changed using this menu.

PLAYBACK FOLDER OPTIONS

D7200	Displays images in all folders created by the D7200.
All (default)	Displays images in all folders on the memory card.
Current	Displays images in the current folder only.

› Hide image

Hidden images are invisible in normal playback, and are protected from deletion (except when you format the memory card(s)). They can only be seen through this menu.

The procedure for selecting images to hide is the same as selecting images for deletion, except that the images you select are tagged with ▨.

› Playback display options

This important menu lets you choose what (if any) information about each image will be displayed on playback, over and above the bare-bones info screen that is always available. As such, these options have already been described on page 96.

› Copy image(s)

This menu item allows image(s) recorded on one memory card to be copied to the other card (assuming both card slots are in use and there is space on the destination card). **Select source** determines which card images will be copied from; the other card then automatically becomes the destination. **Select image(s)** allows individual images or entire folders to be selected for copying. **Select destination folder** determines which folder on the destination card will be used or lets you create a new one.

> **Tip**
>
> *It's certainly worth backing up images, but this is a painfully slow way to do it. Instead, consider enabling automatic backup of all images as they are taken (see Role played by card in Slot 2 in the Photo Shooting menu, page 107).*

› Image review

If Image review is **ON**, new images are automatically displayed on the monitor after shooting. If **OFF**, images are only displayed by pressing ▶ .

› After delete

Determines what happens next after you delete an image in normal playback. **Show next** means that the next image in order of shooting will be displayed. **Show previous** means that the previous image in order of shooting will be displayed. **Continue as before** means that display order is determined by the order in which you were viewing images before deleting: if you were scrolling back through the sequence, the previous image will be displayed, and vice versa.

› Rotate tall

Determines whether portrait format ("tall") images are displayed the "right way up" during playback. It's **OFF** by default, which means these images aren't rotated and you need to turn the camera through 90° to view them correctly. If it's **ON**, these images will be correctly orientated but will appear smaller.

› Slide show

Lets you display images as a slide show on the camera's own screen or through a TV. All images (except hidden ones) in the folder or folders selected for playback (see **Playback Folder**, page 102) will be played in chronological order. Before starting, ensure the playback screen is set to **Image only** for an uncluttered slide show.

You can choose a **Frame interval** of **2**, **3**, **5**, or **10** seconds. Select **Start** and press ⊛. When the show ends, a dialog is displayed. Select **Restart** and press ⊛ to play again. You can also return to the Frame interval dialog or exit.

If you press ⊛ during the slide show, the show is paused and the same dialog screen appears, but if you select **Restart** and press ⊛, the show resumes where it left off.

› DPOF print order

This lets you select JPEG image(s) to be printed when the camera is connected to, or the memory card is inserted into, a printer that complies with the DPOF (Digital Print Order Format) standard. If there are no JPEG images on the memory card this menu item is unavailable.

In the **Select/set** screen, choose image(s) to be printed, using the same basic procedure as described on page 102 under **Delete**. Selected images are tagged with 🖶 and the number 01. To print more than one copy of a selected image, hold 🔍🎞 and press ▲ as many times as necessary; the number increases accordingly.

When all desired images have been selected, press ⊙ĸ.

From the confirmation screen select **Print shooting data** if you wish shutter speed and aperture to be shown on all pictures printed. Select **Print date** if you wish the date of the photo to be shown. To confirm the order, press ⊙ĸ.

PICTURE PERFECT ⌄
Enabling image review gives instant feedback—but it can increase battery drain, an important consideration on long days in remote areas. *28mm, 1/250 sec., f/5.6, ISO 200.*

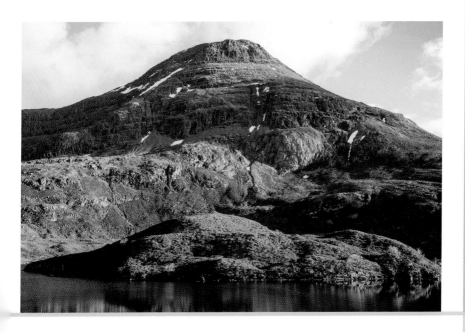

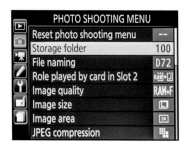

The Photo Shooting menu contains numerous options, but many are more easily accessible through other means and have already been discussed.

› Reset photo shooting menu

This can quickly restore Photo Shooting menu settings to the camera's original default settings. Use with caution as it will wipe out settings that you have carefully chosen.

› Storage folder

By default the D7200 stores images in a single folder (named "100D7200"). If you use multiple memory cards they will all carry folders of the same name. This isn't usually a problem but you might wish to avoid it. You might also want to create dedicated folders for specific shoots or subject types. On extended trips, when you may be storing thousands of images on high-capacity memory cards, creating an

ordered series of folders may be helpful. Only the first three digits are editable and only numbers can be used.

To create a new folder number
1) Select **Select folder by number** and press ⊛.

2) Edit the folder number: press ◀ or ▶ to highlight a digit, ▲ or ▼ to change it. (If the indicated number is already in use, a "blocked folder" icon appears.)

3) Press ⊛ to create a new folder. It automatically becomes the active folder.

To change the active folder
1) Select **Select folder from list** and press ⊛.

2) Select the desired folder and press ⊛.

› File naming

By default, images are named as follows: if they use sRGB color space the name begins "DSC_"; if they use AdobeRGB it begins "_DSC". This is followed by a four-digit number and a three-letter extension (".JPG" for JPEG files, ".NEF" for RAW files).

You can edit the initial three-letter string. As many cameras pass through my hands, I use it to help identify them:

e.g. for images taken on the D7200 I use "D72".

> **Tip**
>
> *The method of text entry described here is used for other functions like Image comment and Copyright information.*

To edit the file-naming string
1) Select **File naming** and press ⊙κ.

2) Edit the three-digit string, using the multi-selector to navigate the "keyboard". To insert the highlighted character press ⊙κ. To make corrections, move the cursor by holding ⊕▦ and pressing ◀ or ▶ ; press 🗑 to delete a character.

3) Press ⊙κ to accept the new name, **MENU** to exit without applying the change.

› Role played by card in Slot 2

When both slots hold memory cards, Slot 2 can be used in three ways. By default (**Overflow**), images are only recorded to Slot 2 when the card in Slot 1 is full. **Backup** means that each image is written to both cards simultaneously.

RAW Slot 1 - JPEG Slot 2 is slightly more complicated. If Image quality is **NEF (RAW)+JPEG**, then the NEF version of each shot is recorded to Slot 1 and the JPEG version to Slot 2. At other Image quality settings, this option behaves like **Backup**.

› Image quality

Choose Image quality options, as described on page 71.

› Image size

Select image size, as described on page 72. If RAW is selected for Image quality this item is grayed out and cannot be accessed.

› JPEG compression

Choose how JPEG images are compressed. **Size priority** means all images are compressed down to a set size (dependent on settings for Image area, Image quality, and Image size). **Optimal quality** means that image sizes are allowed to vary, allowing for better file quality.

› NEF (RAW) recording

Governs how NEF (RAW) files are recorded. See also page 70.

Type gives two options for RAW file compression. The default is **Lossless compressed**: RAW files are compressed by about 20–40% with no detectable effect on image quality. If you select **Compressed**, files are compressed by around 40–55%, with a small effect on image quality.

NEF (RAW) bit depth allows you to select between 12-bit or 14-bit depth. See page 70.

› White balance

Set White balance. See pages 66–69.

› Set Picture Control and Manage Picture Control

These menus govern the use of Nikon Picture Controls. See pages 83–85.

› Color space

Choose between sRGB and Adobe RGB color spaces. See page 70.

› Active D-Lighting

Governs Active D-Lighting. See page 83.

› HDR (high dynamic range)

Enable and control HDR shooting. See page 85.

› Vignette control

Vignetting is darkening towards the corners of the image, most obvious in clear skies and other even-toned areas. Almost all lenses show slight vignetting at maximum aperture. It usually reduces or disappears when the lens is stopped down. In-camera processing of JPEG images (not RAW files or movies) can compensate for vignetting. It only applies with DX lenses of Type D, G, or E.

Choose between **Normal** (the default setting), **High**, **Low**, and **Off**.

› Auto distortion control

If **On**, this automatically corrects for distortion arising with certain lenses. It's available only with Type G, D, or E lenses, excluding fisheye lenses. It only applies to JPEG images, not RAW images or movies.

› Long exposure NR

Photos taken at long shutter speeds can suffer from increased noise so extra image processing is available to counteract this. If Long exposure noise reduction (NR) is **On**, it operates when exposure times are longer than 1 second. During processing, **Job nr** blinks in the displays. You can't take another picture until processing is complete; the delay is roughly equal to the shutter speed in use. Because of the delay, many users prefer to tackle image noise in post-processing. Long exp. NR is **Off** by default.

› High ISO NR

Photos taken at high ISO settings can also show significant noise. The default setting is **Normal**. Other options are **Low** or **High**. High ISO NR can also be set to **Off**, but a modest amount of NR is still applied to JPEG images taken at the highest ISO settings.

Setting	Description
📷⌚ Delayed remote	Shutter fires approximately 2 sec. after ML-L3 is tripped.
📷 Quick response remote	Shutter fires immediately when ML-L3 is tripped.
Remote mirror-up	Press ML-L3 once to raise the mirror; press it again to take the picture.
Off	Camera does not respond to ML-L3.

› ISO sensitivity settings

Governs ISO settings. See page 56.

› Remote control mode (ML-L3)

Unlike some other Nikon DSLRs, there is no dedicated remote control position on the Release mode dial, so you must visit this menu in order to use the ML-L3 remote control with the D7200 (see table on the left).

If you don't use the ML-L3 for a while, the setting will revert to **Off**, and you'll need to revisit this menu to use the ML-L3 again. To determine the interval before this happens, use Custom Setting c5.

› Multiple exposure

When you can merge images on the computer, precisely and flexibly, in-camera multiple exposure may appear unnecessary. However, the Nikon manual states *"multiple exposures produce colors noticeably superior to those in software-generated photographic overlays."* This is debatable, especially if you shoot RAW and process carefully before merging on the computer, but this feature does offer an effective way to combine images for immediate use, e.g. as JPEG files for printing.

To create a multiple exposure

1) Select **Multiple exposure mode** and press ▶. Select **On (series)** to keep shooting multiple exposures or **On (single photo)** to shoot just one. Press ⓄⓀ.

2) Select **Number of shots** and choose **2** or **3**. Press ⓄⓀ.

3) Select **Auto gain** and choose **ON** or **OFF** (see explanation below). Press ⓄⓀ.

4) Frame the first photo and shoot normally. In continuous release modes, the images will be exposed in a single burst. In single-frame release mode, one image will be exposed at each press of the shutter-release button. Normally the maximum interval between shots is 30 sec. You can extend this by setting a longer delay in Custom setting c2.

Auto gain

Auto gain (**On** by default) adjusts the exposure, so that if you are shooting a sequence of three shots, each is exposed at ⅓ the exposure value required for a single exposure. You might turn it **Off** where a moving subject is well lit but the background is dark, so that the subject is well exposed and the background isn't over-lightened.

› Interval timer shooting

The D7200 can take a number of shots at pre-determined intervals. These can be used in various ways, including the creation of time-lapse movies (this requires dedicated software).

1) Select **Start options** and press ▶. Use the multi-selector to set the date and time of the start (up to a week ahead), or select **Now**. Press ⓄⓀ.

2) Select **Interval** and press ▶. Use the multi-selector to set the interval between shots (the default is 1 minute). Press ⓄⓀ.

3) Select **No of intervalsxshots/interval** and press ▶. Use the multi-selector to set the number of intervals and the number of shots to be taken at each interval. The screen shows the total number of shots. Press ⓄⓀ.

4) Select **Exposure smoothing** and choose **Off** or **On**. Exposure smoothing aims to minimize brightness differences between successive shots. Press ⓄⓀ to complete setup and return to the primary Interval timer shooting screen.

5) Highlight **Start>On** and press ⓄⓀ. If you selected **Now** under **Start** options, shooting begins in about 3 sec.

» MOVIE SHOOTING MENU

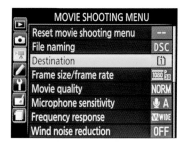

Many of the Movie Shooting menu options are identical to or very similar to those in the Photo Shooting menu and as such have already been discussed.

› Reset movie shooting menu

Resets all options in this menu to original default values.

› File naming

Sets naming options for movie files, just as with stills. The default for the initial three-letter string is "DSC", which you can change; the extension is "MOV", which you can't change.

› Destination

Determines which card slot is used for recording movies. Unlike stills, you cannot record movies to both slots simultaneously. It may make sense to use one card for stills

and one for movies. The settings screen shows available recording time for each card at current settings.

› Frame size/frame rate

Selects the frame size for movies: either 1920 x 1080 pixels (Full HD), denoted **1080p**, or 1280 x 720 pixels, denoted **720p**. The frame rate options vary according to the size chosen.

› Movie quality

Sets the compression level; options are **High** or **Normal**. Note: footage recorded to card is always compressed to some degree, though High quality is fine for most purposes (akin to JPEG Fine for stills).

› Microphone sensitivity

Determines the sensitivity of the built-in microphones (or an external microphone if attached).

› Frequency response

Again this applies both to the built-in microphones or an external one. **Wide range** (the default) picks up a broad frequency range which may capture all kinds of ambient sound. **Vocal range** is tailored more narrowly to the normal frequencies of human speech and can give cleaner sound when recording dialog.

› Wind noise reduction

This applies only to the built-in microphones. Enabling it can indeed reduce the level of wind noise but may also impair the quality of other sound.

› Image area

Determines whether movies use the full width of the sensor, denoted DX, or a smaller **1.3x** area. See page 72.

› White balance

Sets white balance for movie shooting. The procedure, and the options, are just the same as for stills, except for one extra item, **Same as photo settings**. This will match movie white balance to the current still photography setting.

› Set Picture Control and Manage Picture Control

Again, these are exactly equivalent to corresponding items in the Photo Shooting menu, except for the addition of **Same as photo settings**.

› High ISO NR

Does the same job as the corresponding item in the Photo Shooting menu.

› Movie ISO sensitivity settings

In almost all shooting modes, ISO control is automatic. However, if you shoot in mode M you can set the ISO yourself using **ISO sensitivity (mode M)**. You can also opt for **Auto ISO control (mode M)**. This works in the same way as Auto ISO sensitivity control in stills shooting. Finally, **Maximum sensitivity** lets you set an upper limit to the ISO which auto control can set—options run from **200** to **Hi2**.

› Time-lapse photography

Time-lapse photography shoots a series of still frames and combines them into a silent movie. Camera setup is similar to Interval timer photography and it's advisable to start with a fully charged battery or mains adapter.

1) Select **Time-lapse photography** and press ▶.

2) Select **Interval** and press ▶. The default interval between shots is 5 sec.; change this using the multi-selector. Press ⓞⓚ.

3) Choose the **Shooting time**. The default is 25 minutes; use the multi-selector to change this. The maximum you can set is 7 hrs 59 min. Press ⓞⓚ.

4) Select **Exposure smoothing** and choose **Off** or **On**. Exposure smoothing aims to minimize brightness differences between successive shots. Press ⓞⓚ.

5) In the main Time-lapse photography screen, select **Start** and press ⓞⓚ to proceed; shooting begins after about 3 sec.

For more sophisticated time-lapse, shoot RAW or JPEG using the Interval timer and use dedicated software to combine them into a movie.

OPENING SEQUENCE ⌄
A flower opening is a perfect subject for a time-lapse sequence but it would have to stretch over a few days and will require controlled lighting. *100mm macro, 1/200 sec., f/11, ISO 400, tripod.*

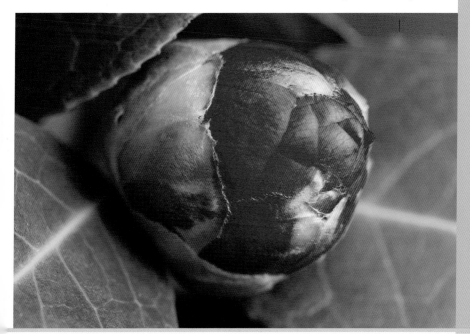

› a: Autofocus

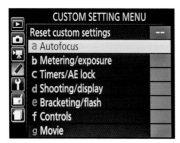

CUSTOM SETTING MENU
Reset custom settings   --
a Autofocus
b Metering/exposure
c Timers/AE lock
d Shooting/display
e Bracketing/flash
f Controls
g Movie

The Custom Setting menu allows you to fine-tune almost every aspect of the camera's operation to suit your personal preferences. There are seven submenus, identified by key letters and a color:
a: Autofocus (red); **b: Metering/Exposure** (yellow); **c: Timers/AE Lock** (green); **d: Shooting/display** (light blue); **e: Bracketing/flash** (dark blue); **f: Controls** (lilac); and **g: Movie** (purple).

Navigating the Custom Setting menu is broadly similar to the other menus. However, from the main menu screen, the first press on ▶ takes you into the list of submenus. Scroll through these to the desired group and press ▶ to see its items.

Once in this list, individual menu items appear in a continuous list, so you can scroll from a9 to b1, and so on. Scrolling up, you can jump directly from from a1 to g4.

The identifying code (e.g. a4) is shown in the appropriate color for that group. If you change the setting from default value, an asterisk appears over the initial letter.

a1 AF-C priority selection and a2 AF-S priority selection
Normally, in AF-C (Continuous-servo) release mode, the camera can take a picture even if it has not acquired perfect focus (**release priority**). Custom setting a1 lets you choose **focus priority** instead, meaning that pictures can only be taken once focus is acquired. Similarly, Custom setting a2 lets you change the priority setting for AF-S (Single-servo AF), but the default is **focus priority**.

a3 Focus tracking with lock-on
This governs how rapidly the camera reacts to sudden large changes in the distance to the subject. If this is **Off**, the camera reacts instantly to such changes, but this means it can be fooled when other objects pass in front of the subject. Longer delays reduce its sensitivity to such intrusions. Options run from **5 (Long)** via **3 (Normal)**, which is the default, to **1 (Short)** as well as **Off**.

a4 AF activation
Determines how you activate autofocus. By default (**Shutter/AF-ON**) you can do so by half-pressing the shutter-release button. If you select **AF-ON** only instead, you must use another button to do so. This can be Fn, Pv, or (most likely) **AE-L/AF-L**. This allows you to use back-button AF, as described on page 79.

a5 Focus point illumination

This determines whether the active focus point is illuminated in red in the viewfinder. If not, it's outlined in black instead. The default is **Auto**, which means the focus point is illuminated only when this will give better contrast with the background. Alternatively, it can be **On** or **Off**.

You can also choose whether or not the focus point(s) are illuminated when you're using Manual focus. They are useful if using focus confirmation but otherwise can be a distraction.

a6 Focus point wrap-around

This governs whether the active focus point can "jump" to the opposite edge of the available area (see page 76). The options are **Wrap** or **No wrap** (default).

a7 Number of focus points

This governs the number of focus points you'll see when selecting the focus point manually. By default it uses all **51 points** but you can opt to use just **11 points** to speed up selection.

> **Note:**
> Even with **11 points** selected here, the camera still uses all 51 points for automatic selection, focus tracking, and so on.

a8 Store points by orientation

This enables the camera to remember different selections for the initial placement of the focus point according to the orientation of the camera. You might use this in fast-moving shooting where you want to switch quickly between two views. For example, when shooting running or cycling, you'll often want to use the uppermost focus point to focus on a competitor's face as this is usually high in the frame—but what counts as "high in the frame" changes according to whether the camera is in portrait or landscape orientation. To enable this function, select **Yes** in this menu.

a9 Built-in AF-assist illuminator

This determines whether the AF-assist illuminator operates when lighting is poor: options are **On** (default) or **Off**.

> **Tip**
>
> *If there are certain Custom settings that you visit frequently (e.g. for me, c3 Self-timer), these can be accessed more rapidly via Recent Settings; better still, opt for My Menu and add them to the list there.*

b1 ISO sensitivity step value

This governs the increments used when changing ISO sensitivity value; options are ⅓ **step** (default) or ½ **step**.

b2 EV steps for exposure cntrl

This governs the increments that the camera uses for setting shutter speed and aperture, as well as for bracketing, exposure compensation, and so on. Again, options are ⅓ **step** (default) or ½ **step**.

b3 Easy exposure compensation

This determines how you can apply exposure compensation in P, S, and A modes. When it's **Off** (the default setting), you must press ⭾ and rotate the main command dial. When it's **On**, you can apply exposure compensation simply by rotating the sub-command dial (P and S modes) or main command dial (A mode).

Auto reset means that compensation set in this way returns to **Off** when the camera or meter turns off. (Settings made using ⭾ still don't reset automatically.)

b4 Center-weighted area

This governs the size of the predominant area when Center-weighted metering is in use. The default size is **8mm**; alternatives are **6mm**, **10mm**, and **13mm**. **Average** means the camera meters equally from the entire image area.

b5 Fine tune optimal exposure

This allows for a sort of permanent exposure compensation; you can apply separate settings for each of the three metering methods (Matrix, Center-weighted, and Spot), in steps of ⅙ Ev, up to +/−1 Ev.

Usually the regular exposure compensation procedure is preferable, but this option could be useful for specific needs. You may, for example, prefer portraits to have a consistently lighter feel, and could adjust the center-weighted setting for this purpose.

You will need to remember that this is in effect as the normal exposure compensation indicator is not displayed; you can only confirm the setting by revisiting this menu.

SELF-TIMER »

I find self-timer sequences very handy when walking or cycling alone. Shooting several frames at 0.5-second intervals—like those composited here—gives a reasonable chance that one or two will be keepers.
18mm, 1/500 sec., f/7.1, ISO 400.

c1 Shutter-release button AE-L

This determines whether you can lock exposure by half-pressure on the shutter-release button. By default, this item is **Off**; half-pressure locks focus only (see Focus lock, page 78), and you can only lock exposure with **AE-L/AF-L**.

c2 Standby timer

This governs the interval before the exposure meter turns off when the camera is idle (i.e. you don't take any pictures, or operate any of the other controls). A shorter delay benefits battery life.

The default is **6 sec.**; alternatives range from **4 sec.** to **30 minutes**. **No limit** means the meter remains active until you turn the camera off.

c3 Self-timer

This has three submenus governing the operation of the self-timer.

Self-timer delay determines the interval between pressing the button and the shot being taken. The default is **10 sec.**; alternatives are **2**, **5**, and **20 sec.**

You can take a single shot, or shoot several with one press of the release button.

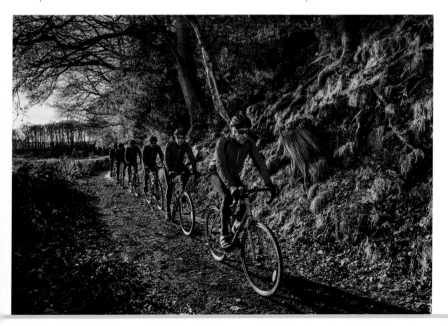

Number of shots can be set from **1–9**, and **Interval between shots** can be set to **0.5**, **1**, **2**, or **3 sec.**

c4 Monitor off delay

Governs how long the LCD monitor screen remains illuminated when the camera is idle. Shorter delays improve battery economy. You can set the delay separately for **Playback**, **Menus**, **Information display**, **Image review**, and **Live view**. For most, the options range from **4 sec.** to **10 mins.** For Image review there's also a **2 sec.** option. For Live View the range is **5 min** to **30 min**, plus **No limit**.

c5 Remote on duration (ML-L3)

When using the optional ML-L3 remote control, this governs how long the camera will remain on standby for a signal from the remote before remote control mode turns **Off**. Options range from **1 min** (default) to **15 min**. Shorter delays improve battery economy.

d1 Beep

If you wish, the camera can emit a beep when the self-timer operates, and to signify focus acquisition when shooting in AF-S mode. It is (rightly!) **Off** by default.

There are two submenus. **Volume** includes the **Off** setting; enable the beep by selecting **1**, **2**, or **3**. Pitch can be **High** or **Low**.

d2 Continuous low speed

This governs the frame rate when using C$_L$ release mode. The default is **3fps** (frames per second), and options run from **1** to **6fps**—though 6fps seems pointless, as it makes C$_L$ identical to C$_H$.

d3 Maximum continuous release

This determines the maximum number of shots that you can take in a single burst when using C$_L$ or C$_H$ release mode. The upper limit is **100**. You can take it down to 1 if you wish, but that rather defeats the object of continuous release mode.

> **Note:**
> The 100-shot limit applies when shooting JPEG images. Buffer capacity imposes much lower burst limits when shooting RAW images.

d4 Exposure delay mode

You can create a delay of **1s**, **2s**, or **3s** when you press the shutter release. This is a possible alternative to the self-timer or mirror lock-up to reduce vibration when shooting on a tripod. It's **Off** by default.

d5 Flash warning

In P, S, A, or M modes, determines whether the flash-ready symbol will blink in the viewfinder to indicate that flash may be required. It's **On** by default. (In other modes flash either activates automatically or remains off.)

d6 File number sequence

This controls how image numbers are set. If it's **Off**, file numbering is reset to 0001 whenever you insert a new memory card, format an existing card, or create a new storage folder. If it's **On**—which is the default—numbering continues from the previous highest number used. **Reset** creates a new folder and begins numbering from 0001.

d7 Viewfinder grid display

This allows the camera to display grid lines in the viewfinder; these can help you keep the camera level and assist with precise framing. The options are **Off** (default) and **On**. It's a personal choice, but I always enable the grid.

d8 Easy ISO

This lets you change the ISO setting simply by rotating one of the command dials. In A mode, you use the main command dial; in S or P mode you use the sub-command dial. You can't use it in Manual, when both command dials are required for their primary purpose, or any other mode. It's **Off** by default.

d9 Information display

Determines the appearance of the information display. By default (**Auto**) the camera switches automatically from **Dark on light** to **Light on dark** to suit lighting conditions, but you can opt to apply one or the other at all times.

> **Note:**
> You can't engage both d8 Easy ISO and b3 Easy exposure compensation, as both require use of the same dial.

3

d10 LCD illumination

This governs illumination of the top-plate control panel. By default (**Off**), it only illuminates when you move the power switch to ☀. **On** means it is illuminated whenever the exposure meter is active. Clearly, **Off** is better for battery life.

d11 MB-D15 battery type

If you're using an optional MB-D15 battery pack with AA batteries, set this to match battery type: **LR6 (AA alkaline)**, **HR6 (AA Ni-MH)**, or **FR6 (AA lithium)**.

d12 Battery order

Again, this applies when using an MB-D15 battery pack. It determines whether the camera will draw on its own internal battery first, or on those in the MB-D15. The latter is the default.

› e: Bracketing/flash

e1 Flash sync speed

This determines the fastest flash sync speed (see page 152 for an explanation). Settings run from **1/250s** (the default) down to **1/60s**.

There are also settings of **1/320s (Auto FP)** and **1/250s (Auto FP)** (see High speed flash sync, page 157).

e2 Flash shutter speed

The previous item controls the fastest shutter speed which can be used with flash. This one determines the slowest shutter speed which the camera can set when using flash in P or A exposure modes. The options run from 1/60 sec. (default) to 30 sec. in 1 Ev steps. In M or S modes, any speed down to 30 sec. can be set anyway.

e3 Flash cntrl for built-in flash

This governs control of the built-in flash (see table opposite).

e4 Exposure comp. for flash

Determines how exposure compensation operates when flash is active. If you select **Background only**, the compensation setting only affects the ambient exposure; flash output is unchanged. If **Entire frame** is selected (which is the default), flash output is increased or reduced by the same amount.

e5 Modeling flash

Applies when the built-in flash is active or you attach a compatible optional flash unit. If it's **On** (which is the default), the flash emits a pulse of light when you press the Pv button, giving an indication of the flash effect. It's limited, but you can gauge where shadows fall.

e6 Auto bracketing set

Bracketing is discussed in detail on page 63. The options are: **AE & flash** (default), **AE only**, **Flash only**, **WB bracketing**, and **ADL bracketing**.

e7 Bracketing order

Determines the order in which auto-bracketed exposures are taken: by default, the first exposure is taken at the metered exposure (**MTR > under > over**). The alternative (**Under > MTR > over**) takes the three shots in ascending sequence (like the images on page 158), which seems more logical.

Main setting	Explanation	Sub-menu options
TTL (default)	Flash output is regulated automatically by the camera's metering system.	
Manual	You determine the strength of the flash.	From Full power to 1/128.
Repeating flash	Fires the flash multiple times during a single exposure, giving a stroboscopic effect.	Output (flash power). Times (no. of flashes). Frequency (no. of flashes per second).
Commander mode	Uses the built-in flash as a trigger for remote flash unit(s) (see page 159).	Set mode and Compensation for Built-in flash and external units/groups; select Group and Channel for external units.

3

› f: Controls

f1 OK button

This menu allows the ⊗ button to perform some additional functions.

Custom Setting f1	OK button
Options—shooting mode	Select center focus point (default)
	Highlight active focus point
	None
Options—playback mode	Thumbnail on/off (default)
	View histograms
	Zoom on/off
	Choose slot and folder
Options—Live View	Select center focus point (default)
	Zoom on/off
	None

f2 Assign Fn button

Various functions can be assigned to the Fn button, on its own or in conjunction with the command dials. These include functions which are normally assigned to other buttons (e.g. depth of field preview, normally assigned to the Pv button). There are separate lists of options for a simple press and for using the button in conjunction with a command dial; however, many options in the two lists are incompatible. If you pick a **Press** option that is incompatible with the one you picked under **Press + command dials**, your prior choice is deactivated, and a message is displayed.

f2 Assign Fn button: Press

Preview	Fn activates depth of field preview.
FV lock	Fn locks flash value (compatible flashguns only): see page 154. Press again to cancel.
AE/AF lock	Exposure and focus both lock when you press Fn.
AE lock only	Exposure locks while you hold Fn.
AE lock (Hold)	Exposure locks when you press Fn and remains locked until you press it again, or standby timers expire.
AF lock only	Focus locks when you press Fn.
AF-ON	Pressing Fn activates focus: focus can't be activated with half-press on shutter release.
🚫	Flash will not fire while Fn is pressed.
Bracketing burst	Fn activates a bracketing burst at last used settings.
+NEF (RAW)	When Image quality is set to JPEG, pressing Fn ensures a NEF copy of the next shot will also be recorded.
Matrix metering	Hold Fn to activate matrix metering.
Center-weighted metering	Hold Fn to activate center-weighted metering.
Spot metering	Hold Fn to activate spot metering.
Viewfinder grid display	Press Fn to show/hide framing grid in viewfinder.
Viewfinder virtual horizon	Press Fn to show a virtual horizon in viewfinder.
MY MENU	Press Fn to display My Menu.
Access top item in My Menu	Press Fn to go straight to Item 1 in My Menu.
Playback	Fn duplicates function of ▶.
NONE (default)	Pressing Fn has no effect.

f2 Assign Fn button: Press

Choose Image area (default)	Press Fn and rotate either command dial to select FX, 1.2x, 5:4, or DX image areas. You can also use this menu item to uncheck any of the available areas in this list: e.g. uncheck 1.2x and 5:4 so that using Fn and dial simply toggles between FX and DX.

f2 Assign Fn button: Press + Command dials

1 step spd/aperture	If Fn is pressed while command dials are rotated, changes to aperture/shutter speed are made in 1 Ev steps.
Choose non-CPU lens number	Use Fn and either command dial to select among lenses specified using Non-CPU lens data.
Active D-Lighting	Press Fn and rotate either command dial to select Active D-Lighting options.
HDR (high dynamic range)	Press Fn and rotate main command dial to choose HDR mode (single photo or series). Press Fn and rotate sub-command dial to choose HDR strength.
Exposure delay mode	Press Fn and rotate either command dial to select an exposure delay.
NONE (default)	Rotating a command dial while pressing Fn has no effect.

f3 Assign Preview button

The same wide range of functions can be assigned to the Preview button as to the Fn button (above). The only difference is in the default settings.

For **Press**, the default setting (not surprisingly!) is **Preview**.

For **Press + Command dials**, the default setting) is **None**. As with f2, if you pick an incompatible **Press** option, **Press + command dials** is deactivated, and vice versa.

f4 Assign AE-L/AF-L button

You can also assign various functions to the **AE-L/AF-L** button. Again, there are incompatibilities between the two lists.

f4 Assign *AE-L/AF-L* button: Press

Options		
	AE/AF lock (default)	Pressing **AE-L/AF-L** locks both focus and exposure until next shot is taken.
	AE lock only	Pressing **AE-L/AF-L** locks exposure until next shot is taken.
	AE lock (Hold)	Pressing **AE-L/AF-L** locks exposure for all subsequent shots, until you press it again or the standby timer interval runs out.
	AF lock only	Pressing **AE-L/AF-L** locks focus until next shot is taken.
	AF-ON	Pressing **AE-L/AF-L** activates focus: focus can't be activated with half-press on shutter release.
	FV lock	Pressing **AE-L/AF-L** locks flash value (built-in and compatible flashguns only).
	None	Pressing **AE-L/AF-L** has no effect.

f4 Assign *AE-L/AF-L* button: Press + Command dials

Options		
	Choose Image area	Press **AE-L/AF-L** and rotate a command dial to toggle between DX and 1.3x crop.
	Choose non-CPU lens number	Press **AE-L/AF-L** and rotate a command dial to select among lenses specified using Non-CPU lens data.
	None	Rotating a command dial while pressing **AE-L/AF-L** has no effect.

f5 Customize command dials

You can change the operation of the command dials in various ways. There are five submenus.

Reverse rotation

This reverses the effect of rotating the dials in a given direction. You can customize this separately for **Exposure compensation** and for **Shutter speed/aperture** settings.

Change main/sub

Normally, when shooting in modes **A**, **S**, and **M**, the main command dial sets shutter speed and sub-command dial sets aperture; this item modifies these roles. Under **Exposure setting**, **On** reverses the usual roles completely. Alternatively, you can select **On (mode A)** to use the main command dial for aperture selection in mode A, while retaining normal operation in other modes.

Similarly, under **Autofocus setting**, you can reverse the normal effect of rotating the command dials while holding ⊙. If this is **On**, holding ⊙ and rotating main command dial selects AF-area mode, ⊙ and sub-command dial selects AF mode.

Aperture setting

This determines whether the aperture ring on older lenses can be used to set apertures, or the sub-command dial (See page 52). On non-CPU lenses, only the aperture ring can be used anyway.

Menus and playback

This lets you use the main command dial to navigate playback images and menus. **On** lets you use it to scroll through individual images in image review and playback. **On (image review excluded)** lets you use the dial only in playback initiated with ▶, not with images displayed immediately after shooting. With either option enabled, the sub-command dial can be used to skip from page to page when images are displayed as thumbnails.

In menu navigation, with either option enabled, the main command dial can be used to scroll through menu items, while the sub-command dial can be used to enter submenus (rotate right) or go up a level (rotate left).

Sub-dial frame advance

This gives the sub-command dial a function during playback. If you're using the main command dial to scroll through images on playback, you can set the sub-command dial to jump forward or back by **10** or **50** images, or to jump to the next **Folder** (if more than one folder exists on the memory card).

f6 Release button to use dial

Normally, buttons such as **QUAL**, **WB** , or **ISO** must be held down while you rotate the appropriate command dial to make changes. If you select **Yes** in this menu, you can continue to make changes after releasing the button.

f7 Slot empty release lock

By default (**OK** selected in this menu), the shutter can be released even with no memory card loaded. Images are held in the buffer and can be displayed on the monitor (demo mode), but are not recorded. As this can allow you to imagine that you are shooting normally even though there's no card to record the images, you can select **LOCK** instead. The default setting is useful when cameras are on display at a shop or trade show—which is why it's the default—but not in normal use. I always change it when I receive a new camera.

f8 Reverse indicators

This governs how the exposure displays in the viewfinder and control panel are shown. By default (**-0+** selected) over-exposure is indicated by bars on the right. **+0-** reverses the indicators.

f9 Assign movie record button

This gives ⊙ a function during normal

photography and still-image Live View. The default is **None**, i.e. the button remains inactive. There are three alternative **Press + command dials** options: **White balance**, **ISO sensitivity**, and **Choose image area**.

f10 Assign MB-D16 AE-L/AF-L button

This lets you allocate a range of a functions to the **AE-L/AF-L** button on the optional MB-D15 battery pack. Most of the options are the same as those available for the camera's own **AE-L/AF-L** button (see Custom setting f4). There is one additional option: **Same as Fn button**. This allows the battery pack's **AE-L/AF-L** button to perform the same function that you've selected for the Fn button on the camera (using Custom setting f2). There is no **None** option and no **Press + command dials** options.

f11 Assign remote (WR) Fn button

Similarly, lets you assign various functions to the Fn button on some Nikon wireless remote controls. The main options are **Preview, FV lock, AE/AF lock, AE lock only, AF lock only, Flash off, +NEF (RAW)**, Lv , and **None**. In addition you can choose **=Fn, =Pv**, or **= AE-L/AF-L** which make the button match the function you've selected for the Fn, Pv, or **AE-L/AF-L** button on the camera.

› g: Movie

This menu lets you assign functions to certain key buttons: these only apply when the camera is in movie mode and can be completely different from the functions performed by the same button when shooting stills.

g1 Assign Fn Button

This governs the function performed by Fn when the camera is in movie mode. The following are available: **AE/AF lock** (default), **AE lock only**, **AE lock (Hold)**, **AF lock only**, **AF-ON**, **FV lock**, **None**. In addition there are two options relevant only to movie shooting.

g1 Assign Fn Button	
Index marking	Press Fn during movie shooting to add an index mark, which can be used to jump to specific points when playing and editing movies.
View photo shooting info	Press Fn to show current still photo settings (shutter speed, aperture, ISO); press again to show current movie settings.

g2 Assign preview button

You can assign exactly the same range of functions to the Pv button, but the default is **Index marking**.

g3 Assign AE-L/AF-L button

You can also assign the same range of functions to **AE-L/AF-L** . The default is **AE/AF lock**.

g4 Assign shutter button

This determines the behavior of the shutter-release button when the Live View selector is set to ![movie icon].

By default (**Take photos**), fully pressing the shutter-release button ends movie recording (if in progress) and takes a still photo (see page 181). Alternatively, you can select **Record movies**. In this case, half-pressure on the button begins Movie Live View (effectively duplicating the function of Lv). Fully pressing the button begins recording a movie clip, and a second press ends it; this effectively duplicates the function of ⦿ . If you're shooting movies seriously, this can streamline operations, but leaves no quick way to capture a still photo. This setting also lets you use a remote cord or wireless remote controller (but not the ML-L3) to start and end movie shooting.

» SETUP MENU

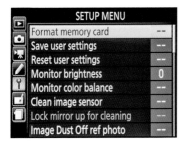

The Setup menu controls various important camera functions, though many are ones you will need to access only occasionally, if at all.

› Format memory card

This is the one item in this menu that you are likely to use regularly. The process is outlined on page 24.

› Save user settings and Reset user settings

See page 88.

› Monitor color balance

Adjust the color balance of the monitor using the multi-selector. When you enter this menu, the screen shows the most recent image taken. However, using a photo for reference can be seriously misleading if the subject is non-average or it was shot using an inappropriate white balance setting. Adjusting screen settings to make it look right then masks the fact that colors in the image itself are wrong, and can throw off your assessment of other images.

If there are no images on the memory card, the screen shows a gray rectangle instead. For the reasons just given, I prefer to use this to judge the color balance of the screen—so I would use this menu when there are no images on the card(s) in the camera. If necessary, simply remove the card(s) for the few seconds it takes to use this menu.

› Clean image sensor and Lock mirror up for cleaning

For details see page 215.

› Image Dust Off ref photo

Nikon Capture NX-D can automatically remove dust spots on images by comparing them to a reference photo which maps dust on the sensor. This can save a lot of "grunt work" compared to manually removing spots from individual images. This menu item lets you take a suitable reference photo.

Taking an Image Dust off ref photo

1) Fit a lens (preferably at least 50mm focal length). With a zoom lens, use the longest setting. Locate a featureless white object such as a sheet of paper, large enough to fill the frame.

2) Select **Image Dust Off Ref Photo** and press ▶.

3) Select **Start** or **Clean sensor and then start** and press ⓞⓚ. (Select **Start** if you have already taken the picture[s] from which you want to remove spots.)

4) Frame the target object at a distance of about 4in. (10cm). Press the shutter-release button halfway; focus is automatically set to infinity, creating a soft white background against which dust spots stand out clearly.

5) Press the shutter-release button fully to capture the reference image.

› Flicker reduction

Some light sources can produce visible flicker in the Live View screen image and in movie recording. To minimize this, use this menu to match the frequency of the local mains power supply. **60Hz** is common in North America; **50Hz** is normal in the European Union, including the UK; the

Auto setting will normally adjust automatically.

› Time zone and date

Sets date, time, and time zone, and specifies the date display format (**Y/M/D**, **M/D/Y**, or **D/M/Y**). Set your home time zone first, then set the time correctly. If you travel to a different time zone, change the time zone setting and the time will be updated automatically.

› Language

Set the language which the camera uses in its menus. The options include most major European and Asian languages.

› Auto image rotation

If set to **ON** (default), information about the orientation of the camera is recorded with every photo taken, ensuring that they will appear right way up when viewed with Nikon View NX-i/Capture NX-D and most third-party imaging applications.

› Battery info

Displays information about battery status, including percentage of charge remaining and how many shots have been taken since the battery was last charged. The information displayed may change if an accessory battery pack is attached.

› Image comment

You can append brief comments (36 characters or about a quarter of a Tweet) to images. Comments appear in the third info page on playback and can be viewed in Nikon View NX-i and Nikon Capture NX-D. To attach a comment, select **Input comment** and press ▶. Use the multi-selector to input text as described on page 106. When finished press ⊙. Select **Attach comment**, then select **Done** and press ⊙. The comment will be attached to all new shots until turned off again.

› Copyright information

Copyright is a fundamental right, and exists automatically in every photo you take. There should be no need to "copyright" images and in most countries you don't need to register them.

However, in the US and a few other countries, registration—although a cumbersome bureaucratic process—can add extra protection.

However, making a clear statement that your images are copyright is still worthwhile. It doesn't confer any additional rights, but may make it easier to enforce the rights you already have.

This menu allows copyright information to be embedded into metadata, using the usual text input method, described on page 106.

There are separate fields for **Artist** (i.e. photographer) and **Copyright**; however, in most jurisdictions, they are usually one and the same person, as copyright automatically belongs to the person creating the image. There is often an exception for photographers shooting in the course of permanent employment (not freelances under contract), when copyright belongs to the employer. Copyright law does vary internationally, and it is wise to familiarize yourself with the local law where you work.

To attach the information to all subsequent photos, select **Attach copyright information**, then press ⊙.

› Save/load settings

This item allows you to save most of your menu settings to a memory card (this must be in Slot 1). If a card containing this settings file is inserted later, these saved settings can be quickly restored. This is useful, for instance, if more than one user share the camera but require many different settings. It can also be used to transfer settings quickly to another D7200, but not to other models. Do not change the name of the settings file or the procedure will fail.

Do not confuse this item with **Save user settings**—though you could be forgiven for doing so! Unlike **Save user settings** the list includes various Playback and Setup menu options, but does not include shooting settings like exposure mode or ISO.

The list includes all Custom settings and most items from the Playback, Photo Shooting, Movie Shooting, and Setup menus, as well as the current state of My Menu/Recent Settings.

› Virtual horizon

Displays a horizon indicator on the monitor to assist in leveling the camera. Green bars indicate when the camera is level.

Unlike models such as the D600 and D800, the D7200's virtual horizon only shows left-to-right tilt (roll); it does not tell you whether the camera is level front–back (pitch). The virtual horizon is still really useful in ensuring that horizons will be level when shooting landscapes and seascapes, for example. However, without a pitch indicator it can't help you keep the camera back vertical, which is the best way to avoid converging verticals when

shooting architecture and similar subjects (see pages 190, 198).

› Non-CPU lens data

Many older Nikon lenses, often rugged and optically excellent, can be used on the D7200. When lenses lack a built-in CPU, little information is available to the camera and shooting options are drastically reduced. Important functions can be restored by specifying the focal length and maximum aperture of a given lens in this menu. Data can be stored for up to nine such lenses.

› AF fine-tune

This menu allows compensation for slight variations in autofocus performance between different lenses (back-focus or front-focus); this applies to CPU lenses only. The camera can store details for several lenses and will subsequently recognize them automatically. This feature should be used with great care and only when you are certain that back-focus or front-focus exists. It is **OFF** by default.

Detecting back-/front-focus requires careful testing. One method is to compare results using standard AF with those from Live View. Use a solid tripod to avoid camera movement and make sure the same focus point is being targeted by both AF systems. For greater precision, test targets are available from several suppliers.

› HDMI

You can connect the camera to HDMI (High Definition Multimedia Interface) TVs and monitors. This menu allows you to set the camera's output to match the HDMI device. See the specifications for the device.

› Location data

Set up a connection with a compatible GPS device (see Chapter 9 Connection).

› Wi-Fi

Use this to enable and regulate the onboard Wi-Fi (see Chapter 9 Connection).

› NFC

Similarly, use this to Enable/Disable NFC connection for devices which support this. (Again, see Chapter 9 Connection.)

› Network

Normally grayed-out and inaccessible, this menu is only used if the camera is connected to Nikon's optional UT-1 communications unit. (See Chapter 8 Accessories and care.)

› Conformity marking

Displays some technical networking standards with which the camera complies. It's for information only; there are no options to choose.

› Firmware version

Firmware is the onboard software which controls the camera's operation. Nikon issues updates periodically. This item shows the version presently installed, so you can verify whether it is current.

When Nikon release new firmware, download it and copy it to a memory card. Insert this card in the camera then use this menu to update the camera's firmware.

Note:
Firmware updates may include new functions and new menu items, which can make this Guide (and the Nikon manual) appear out of date.

3 » RETOUCH MENU

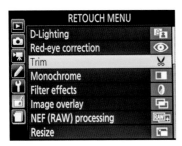

The Retouch menu lets you correct, enhance, and modify images in various ways. Retouching does not affect the original image but creates a copy to which the changes are applied. Further retouch options can be applied to the new copy, with some limitations: for example, you can't normally apply any given effect more than once. Copies are always created in JPEG format but the size and quality depends on the format of the original.

Format of original photo	Quality and size of copy
NEF (RAW)	Fine, Large
JPEG	Quality and size match original

To create a retouched image

1) In the Retouch menu, select a retouch option. If subsidiary options appear, make a further selection. A screen of image thumbnails appears. Select the required image, as you would during normal image playback. A preview of the retouched image appears.

2) Alternatively, from image playback, highlight the image you'd like to retouch. Press ✦ and from the next screen select **Retouch**.

3) Depending on the type of retouching to be done (see below), there may be further options to choose from.

4) Press ⑲ to see a preview of the results. Press ⑲ to create a retouched copy.

> **Note:**
> Retouched copy images are indicated by a ☑ icon in normal image playback.

› Side-by-side comparison

This option is not part of the regular Retouch menu; it is only available in full-frame playback, when you select a retouched copy, or its source image, by pressing ⊞. It displays the copy alongside the original source image. Highlight either image with ◀ or ▶ and press ⊕ to view it full frame. Press ▶ to return to normal playback; to return to the playback screen with the highlighted image selected, press ⊛.

Side-by-side comparison is probably most useful straight after creating a retouched copy, when the copy is displayed on screen, as you can quickly compare the copy with the original image.

› Retouch menu options

D-Lighting

D-Lighting should not be confused with Active D-Lighting, though there are similarities in the final effect. Active D-Lighting is applied before shooting, and has an effect on the original exposure; D-Lighting is applied later and simply lightens the shadow areas of the image. The D-Lighting screen shows the original image and a preview of the retouched version; a press on ⊕ zooms in on this preview. Use ▲ / ▼ to select the strength of the effect—**High**, **Medium**, or **Low**.

Red-eye correction

This tackles the notorious problem of "red-eye", caused by on-camera flash. It can only be selected for photos taken using flash. The camera analyzes the photo for evidence of red-eye; if none is found the process ends. If red-eye is detected a preview image appears; use the zoom controls as usual to view it more closely.

Trim

This lets you crop an image to eliminate unwanted areas or to better fit it to a print size. A preview screen shows the crop area marked by a yellow rectangle. Change the aspect ratio of the crop by rotating the main command dial. Adjust the size of the cropped area by pressing ⊖ to reduce the size, ⊕ to increase it. Adjust its position using the multi-selector. Figures at top left give the

TRIM ⌄
The area of the new image is shown by the yellow rectangle.

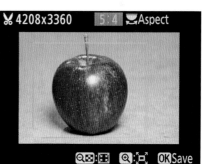

pixel dimensions of the copy. Press (OK) to save a cropped copy.

Monochrome

Create monochrome copies, as straight **Black-and-white**, **Sepia** (a brownish-toned effect), or **Cyanotype** (a bluish-toned effect). For **Sepia** or **Cyanotype**, you can make the toning effect stronger or weaker with ▲ / ▼.

Filter effects

Mimics several common photographic filters (perhaps we should say "once-common" in the days of film). **Skylight** reduces the blue cast which can affect photos taken on clear days with a lot of blue sky. Applied to other images its effect is very subtle, even

MONOCHROME ⌄
A comparison of Sepia (left) and Cyanotype (right). Both effects have been used at the strongest setting.

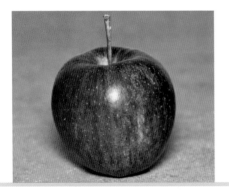

undetectable. **Warm filter** has a much stronger warming effect. **Soft** is also fairly self-explanatory.

Cross screen, however, is an enigmatic name—surely "Star" would have been better? It creates a "starburst" effect around light sources and other very bright points, like sparkling highlights on water. There are multiple options within this item, including the number, angle, and length of the star points.

Image overlay

This lets you create a new combined image from two existing photos (these must be NEF or RAW files). As with multiple exposure, Nikon claim (debatably) that the results are better than combining the images in an application like Photoshop because Image overlay makes direct use of the raw data from the camera's sensor. You can also create a new RAW image by this method—it's the only Retouch menu option which allows you to do this.

To create an overlaid image

1) In the Retouch menu, select **Image overlay** and press ▶. The next screen has panels labeled **Image 1**, **Image 2**, and **Preview**. Initially, **Image 1** is highlighted. Press (OK).

2) The camera displays thumbnails of RAW

Tip

Although Image overlay works from RAW images, the size and quality of the copy are not automatically set to Fine, Large. Make sure the **Image Quality** *and* **Image Size** *options are as required.*

images on the memory card. Select the first image required for the overlay and press (OK). Press ▶ to move to Image 2 and select the second image. You can substitute alternative images in either position as you work through the next steps.

3) Use the Gain control below each image to determine its "weight" in the final overlay.

4) Press ▶ to highlight the Overlay panel. With **Overlay** highlighted, press ⊕ to preview the overlay. Return to the main screen by pressing ⊖ ▦. To save the combined image, highlight **Save** and press (OK).

MONO LITHS

The Retouch menu offers a quick way to make monochrome images.
18mm, 1/125 sec., f/11, ISO 100, tripod.

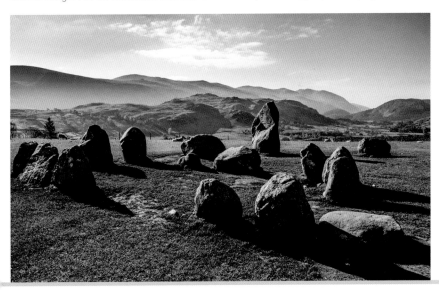

NEF (RAW) processing

This menu creates JPEG copies from images originally shot as RAW files. It's no substitute for full RAW processing on computer, but it does let you create quick copies for previewing or printing. Processing options are displayed in a column alongside a preview image (see table below).

To finish, select **EXE** and press ⊛ to create the JPEG copy. Pressing ▶ exits without creating a copy.

Resize

This option creates a small copy of the selected picture(s), suitable for immediate use with various external devices. Four sizes are available (see table opposite).

When you access Resize from the Retouch menu, you select a picture size first and then select the picture(s) to be copied at that size. When you access from image Playback, you select a picture first and then choose the copy size; this way you can only copy one picture at a time.

Option heading	Description
Image quality	Choose Fine, Normal, or Basic.
Image size	Choose Large, Medium, or Small.
White balance	Choose a white balance setting; options are similar to those described on page 69.
Exposure compensation	Adjust exposure (brightness) levels from +2 to −2.
Set Picture Control	Choose any of the range of Nikon Picture Controls to be applied to the image. Fine-tuning options can also be applied.
High ISO NR	Choose level of noise reduction where appropriate (see page 57).
Color space	Choose color space.
Vignette control	Apply Vignette control.
D-Lighting	Choose D-Lighting level (High, Normal, Low, or Off).

Option	Size (pixels)	Possible uses
2.5M	1920 x 1280	Display on HD TV, larger computer monitor, recent iPads, iPhone 6
1.1M	1280 x 856	Display on typical computer monitor, older iPad
0.6M	960 x 640	Display on standard TV, iPhone 4/5
0.3M	640 x 424	Display on older/simpler mobile devices

Quick retouch

Provides basic "quick fix" retouching, boosting saturation and contrast. D-Lighting is applied automatically to retain shadow detail. Again, you can adjust the strength of the effect, from **Lo** to **Hi**.

Straighten

It's best to get horizons level at the time of shooting, and the virtual horizon can help. However, errors can still happen. This option offers a fall-back, with correction up to 5° in 0.25° steps. Use ▶ to rotate clockwise, ◀ to rotate anticlockwise. Inevitably, this crops the image.

Distortion control

Some lenses create noticeable curvature of straight lines (see page 190); this menu allows you to correct this in-camera. This inevitably crops the image slightly. **Auto** allows automatic compensation for the known characteristics of certain Nikkor lenses; it can't be used on images taken with other lenses. (**Auto Distortion control**, in the Photo Shooting menu, applies this automatically to JPEG images.)

Manual correction can be applied whatever lens was used.

Fisheye

Instead of correcting distortion, this menu exaggerates it to give a (somewhat crude) fisheye lens effect. Use ▶ to strengthen the effect, ◀ to reduce it.

Color outline

This detects edges in the photograph and uses them to create a "line-drawing" effect. There are no options to alter the effect.

COLOR OUTLINE

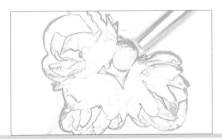

Color sketch

This creates a copy resembling a colored pencil drawing. Controls for **Vividness** and **Outlines** adjust the strength of the effect.

Also available as a Special Effect when shooting.

COLOR SKETCH (VIVIDNESS SET TO MAXIMUM) ⌄

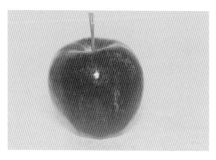

Perspective control

Corrects the convergence of vertical lines in photos taken looking up, for example, at tall buildings. Grid lines help you assess the effect, and you control its strength with the multi-selector. The process inevitably crops the original, so leave room around the subject when you shoot. For alternative approaches to perspective control, and an illustration, see page 198.

Miniature effect

This option mimics the fad—which has already overstayed its 15 minutes of fame—for shooting images with extremely localized depth of field, making real scenes look like miniature models. It usually works best with photos taken from a high viewpoint, which typically have clearer separation of foreground and background. A yellow rectangle shows the area which will remain in sharp focus. You can reposition and resize this using the multi-selector. Press and hold ⊕ to preview the results and press ⊛ to save a retouched copy.

Also available as a Special Effect when shooting.

Selective color

Select up to three specific color(s) to be preserved in the retouched copy, while other hues are transformed to monochrome.

1) Select an image from the thumbnail screen and press ⊛.

2) Use the multi-selector to place the cursor over an area of the desired color. Press ⊛ to choose that color.

3) Turn the main command dial and then use ▲ / ▼ to adjust the color range (i.e. to be more or less selective with the color). A preview shows the effect.

4) To select another color, turn the main command dial again to highlight another "swatch" and repeat steps 2 and 3.

5) To save the image, press (OK).

Also available as a Special Effect when shooting.

Edit movie

This grandly titled item merely allows you to trim the start and/or end of movie clips. It's nothing like proper editing (see page 182), but has its uses.

To trim a movie clip

1) Select a movie clip in full-frame playback (do not play the movie).

2) Press ◄**⧈**►; select **Edit Movie** and press ►.

3) Select **Choose start/end point** and press ►.

4) Press (OK) to start playing the movie. Press ▼ to pause. Rotate the main command dial to jump forward or back in 10-second steps.

5) Press **WB** to toggle between start and end. You can see in the progress bar below the image that the start or end point is highlighted in yellow.

6) Press ▲ to trim the clip at the selected start/end point. Select **Save as new file** and press (OK) to save the trimmed clip as a copy; the original is retained. Or select **Overwrite existing file** and press (OK) to save the trimmed clip in place of the original—use care as this is irrevocable.

7) Repeat if necessary to trim the other end of the clip.

›› RECENT SETTINGS AND MY MENU

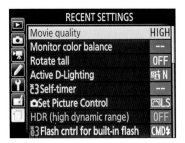

Recent Settings and My Menu share the bottom position in the sidebar of the main menu screen. To choose which is active, follow the **Choose tab** procedure below.

Recent Settings automatically stores the most recent items that you have accessed from any of the other menus, providing a quick way to access controls that you have used recently. The list contains up to 20 items and so is likely to include any that you visit frequently.

My Menu lets you create a customized list of your "favorite" menu items. You do need to add items manually, but it does mean that your preferred items are always there. You can even order them so that your favorites are always at the top. Again, it can store a maximum of 20 items.

› Choose tab

1) In My Menu or Recent Settings (whichever is currently active), select **Choose tab** and press ▶.

2) Select the menu you want to activate and press ⊙к.

› To add items to My Menu

1) Select **Add items** and press ▶.

2) A list of the other menus now appears. Select the appropriate menu and press ▶.

3) Select the desired menu item and press ▶.

4) A **Choose position** screen reappears with the newly added item at the top. Use ▲ / ▼ to reposition it in the list if desired. Press ⊙к to confirm and save the list.

5) Repeat to add more items.

› To remove items from My Menu

1) Select **Remove items** and press ▶.

2) Highlight any item and press ▶ to select it for deletion. A check mark appears beside the item.

3) Select additional items in the same way.

4) Press (ok). A confirmation dialog appears. To confirm the deletion(s) press (ok) again. To exit without deleting anything, press **MENU**.

> ### *Tip*
>
> *A quicker way to delete a single item is to highlight it using the multi-selector, then press 🗑. To confirm deletion press 🗑 again.*

› To rearrange items in My Menu

1) Highlight **Rank items** and press ▶.

2) Highlight any item.

3) Use ▲ or ▼ to move the item up or down; a yellow line shows where its new position will be. Press (ok) to confirm the new position.

4) Repeat steps 2 and 3 to move further items. When finished, press **MENU** to exit.

FLASH

Unlike top pro models like the D4s, the D7200 has a built-in flash. With a short range and ugly light, it has limited value as a main light source. However, it can play a more serious role in providing fill light. It can also act as a "commander" in multi-flash wireless setups, integrating fully into Nikon's Creative Lighting System (CLS). Flash is not the answer for all (or even most?) low-light shots. Understanding its limitations helps us understand when to seek alternatives, as well as when and how to use flash effectively.

» PRINCIPLES

Two facts are fundamental: flashguns are small and flashguns are weak. Built-in units like that on the D7200 and most other DSLRs are especially small and weak—and those on compact cameras even more so.

Being small, the flash produces hard-edged, contrasty light. It's similar to direct sunlight, but even strong sunlight is slightly softened by scattering and reflection; we can use the same principles to soften the flash, too.

The weakness of flash is equally inherent. All flashguns have a limited range. That of on-camera flash is more limited than most accessory flashguns.

Built-in flash units raise a third issue, too. Their fixed position, close to the lens, makes the light one-dimensional—and the same for every shot, which is boring! (See **Built-in flash** on page 146.)

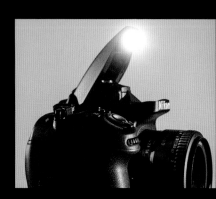

BUILT-IN FLASH ⌃
The built-in pop-up flash is activated by the flash button or automatically by the camera.

FLASH IN THE PAN »
Flash does more than just fill in the shadows here; it gives a sharp image of the rider to set against the motion-blur of the background in this panning shot.
24mm, 1/60 sec., f/13, ISO 100.

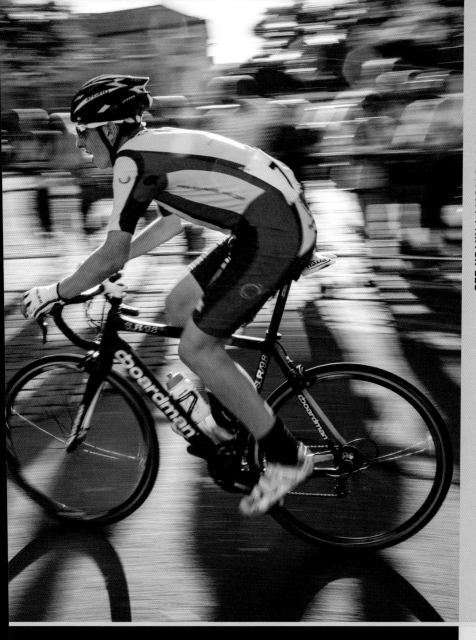

» BUILT-IN FLASH

» FLASH RANGE

Its range is limited, and its light flat and harsh, but the built-in flash is still sometimes better than nothing. However, its real value is for fill light. In 📷ᴬᵁᵀᴼ, and many Scene modes, the flash activates when the camera deems it necessary (Auto flash), though it can always be turned off. In 🚫, and other Scene and Effects modes, the built-in flash is not available.

In P, S, A, or M modes and 🍴, the flash is always available but must be activated manually by pressing ⚡. It then pops up and begins charging. When charged, ⚡ is displayed in the viewfinder. Choose a flash mode as required and take photo(s) in the normal way.

When finished with the built-in flash, press it gently down until it clicks into place.

The range of any flash depends on its power, ISO setting, and the aperture set. The table details the approximate range of the built-in flash for selected apertures and ISO settings. These figures should give a general sense of the limited range that always applies when using flash. A quick test shot will show if a given subject is within range. If not, you can increase effective range by setting a higher ISO and/ or a wider aperture—but only up to a point.

> **Tip**
>
> *The built-in flash covers the field of lenses no wider than 18mm. Some lenses will part-block flash output at close range; removing the lens hood often helps. The Nikon manual details other limitations with certain lenses.*

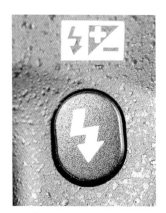

THE ⚡ BUTTON

ISO setting			Range	
100	400	1600	meters	feet
1.4	2.8	5.6	1.0–8.5	3ft 3in.–27ft 11in.
2.8	5.6	11	0.6–4.2	2ft–13ft 9in.
5.6	11	22	0.6–2.1	2ft–6ft 11in.
11	22		0.6–1.1	2ft–3ft 7in.

› Guide Numbers

The Guide Number (GN) indicates the power of a flash. GNs vary with the ISO rating, and can be specified in meters or feet. They can be used to calculate flash exposures and working range, though with modern flash metering this is rarely necessary. GNs also allow comparison of different flashguns. For instance, the GN for the built-in flash is 12 (meters, ISO 100); for the Nikon SB-910 it is 34, indicating almost three times the power. This allows shooting at three times the distance, at a lower ISO, or with a smaller aperture.

SNOW SHADOW ⌄
The built-in flash can throw a very obvious shadow of the lens or lens hood.
12mm, 1/250 sec., f/11, ISO 200.

FLASH RANGE ⌄
The built-in flash lights up the paving in the foreground, and the nearest dancers, but reaches no further.
18mm, 1/40 sec., f/4.5, ISO 3200.

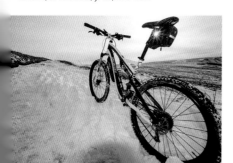

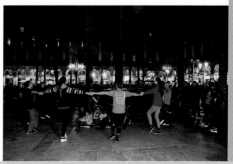

4 » FILL FLASH

A key application for flash is for "fill-in" light, brightening deep shadows like those cast by direct sunlight. Pros may use flash more often in bright sunlight than on duller days.

Fill-flash doesn't need to make the shadows as bright as sunlit areas—that would look very unnatural. Fill-flash can be used at a smaller aperture, or greater distance, than when flash is the main light (typically around 2 Ev smaller, or four times the distance).

In other words, for most setups, fill-flash will almost always apply.

If you use spot metering, Standard i-TTL flash for DSLR applies instead. It treats flash as the main light source, rather than a fill-light. It regulates flash output to light the subject correctly, but doesn't attempt to balance it with ambient illumination.

› i-TTL balanced fill-flash

i-TTL balanced fill-flash helps achieve natural-looking results with fill-in flash. It operates automatically provided (a) matrix or center-weighted metering is selected, and (b) a CPU-equipped lens is attached.

BRING ME SUNSHINE »
Sunlit areas look much the same in both shots, but the fill-flash lightens the shadows.
29mm, 1/250 sec., f/11, ISO 100, tripod.

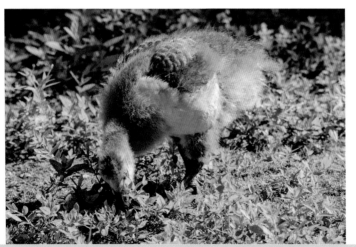

GOSLING «
i-TTL balanced fill-flash for DSLR gives a very natural result; it's not overly obvious that flash has been used at all, but it preserves much more detail in the shadows.
120mm, 1/250 sec., f/11, ISO 200.

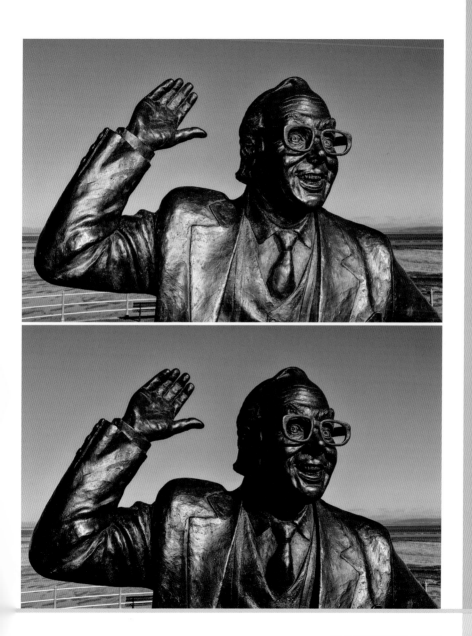

4 » FLASH EXPOSURE

Whether the shutter speed is 1/200 sec. or 20 sec., the flash normally fires just once and delivers the same amount of light to the subject. Therefore, if there is no other light, the subject will look the same at any shutter speed. Of course, shooting in total darkness is not normal; there will nearly always be some other light around, which photographers call ambient light.

When there's any ambient light, shutter speed becomes relevant, as slower shutter speeds give ambient light more chance to register.

Aperture, however, affects both flash and ambient exposure. The camera's flash metering takes this into account but it is useful to understand this distinction for a clearer sense of what's going on, especially with slow-sync shots.

The combinations of shutter speed and aperture that are available when using flash depend on the exposure mode you're using.

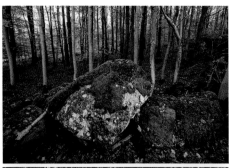

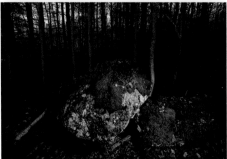

Note:
Under some circumstances flash can be used with shutter speeds faster than 1/250 sec. (see high-speed flash sync, page 157).

LIGHT ROCK 〈〈
Both shots use the same aperture setting, so flash-lit areas in the foreground look essentially the same. However, varying the shutter speed makes a difference in the daylit background. *12mm, 1/10 and 1/40 sec., f/11, ISO 100, tripod.*

EXPOSURE MODE	SHUTTER SPEED	APERTURE
P	Set by camera. The normal range is between 1/250 and 1/60 sec., but in certain flash modes all settings up to 30 sec. are available.	Set by camera.
S	Selected by user. All settings between 1/250 sec. and 30 sec. are available. If you set a faster shutter speed, the D5500 will fire at 1/250 sec. while the flash is active.	Set by camera.
A	Set by camera. The normal range is between 1/250 and 1/60 sec., but in certain flash modes all settings up to 30 sec. are available.	Selected by user.
M	Selected by user. All settings between 1/250 and 30 sec. are available, plus Bulb are available. If you set a faster shutter speed, the shutter is limited to 1/250 sec. while the flash is active.	Selected by user.
![icons] AUTO, 🌷, 🍂, 🌃, 🐕, 🍴, 🏞, 🔲, TOY, VI, POP	Set by camera, between 1/250 and 1/60 sec.	Set by camera.
🎇	Set by camera, between 1/250 and 1/30 sec.	Set by camera.
👤★	Set by camera, between 1/250 and 1 sec.	Set by camera.

» FLASH SYNCHRONIZATION AND FLASH MODES

To cover the whole image frame, flash must fire when the shutter is completely open. However, at faster shutter speeds DSLRs do not expose the whole frame at once. For the D7200, the fastest shutter speed where the entire frame is exposed at once (normally 1/250 sec.) is known as the sync (for synchronization) speed.

Flash modes are distinguished by how they regulate synchronization and shutter speed. To choose flash mode, press 🗲 and rotate the main command dial.

› Standard flash mode (front-curtain sync)

The flash fires as soon as the shutter is fully open, i.e. as soon as possible after the shutter-release button is pressed. In most exposure modes, the camera sets a shutter speed between 1/60 and 1/250 sec.

> **Note:**
> Nikon brands this basic flash mode as "Fill-flash". This is misleading when spot metering is active.

› Slow sync

This mode allows longer shutter speeds (up to 30 sec.) to be used in P and A exposure modes, allowing backgrounds to register even in low ambient light. Movement of the subject and/or camera can create partial blur, combined with a sharp image where the subject is lit by the flash: see photos.

You can't select slow sync in S and M modes, but you don't need to: you can set longer shutter speeds anyway.

› Rear-curtain sync

Unlike front-curtain sync, rear-curtain sync triggers the flash at the last possible instant. With moving subjects, this means that any image created by ambient light appears behind the subject, which usually looks more natural than the alternative.

› Red-eye reduction

Camera-mounted flash often creates "red-eye", caused by light reflecting off the subject's retina. Red-eye reduction works by shining a light (the AF-assist illuminator) at the subject, causing their pupils to contract. This delays the shot, making it unsuitable for moving subjects and killing spontaneity. Generally, it's better to remove red-eye in post-processing or with **Red-eye correction** in the Retouch menu. Alternatively, use bounce or off-camera flash, or up the ISO rating and avoid flash altogether.

Red-eye reduction is the default in ![party icon] Party/indoor, but fortunately flash mode can be changed.

› Red-eye reduction with slow sync

This combines the two modes, allowing backgrounds to register. This may help shots look more natural than red-eye reduction mode alone, but is still subject to delay.

Tips

Shooting with rear-curtain sync gets tricky with longer exposures, as you need to predict where your subject will be at the end of the exposure.

Nikon's documentation refers to "auto flash" modes. These are just the regular modes described here, initiated automatically in Full Auto and certain Scene modes.

FLASH EXPOSURE COMPARISON ❯❯
Slow sync combines a flash image with a motion-blurred image from the ambient light. With front-curtain sync (left) blurred elements, like the headlight traces, appear to run ahead of the sharp flash image. With rear-curtain sync (right), they trail behind it.
28mm, 1/3 sec., f/8, ISO 200.

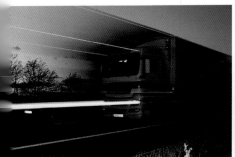
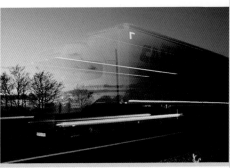

4 » FLASH COMPENSATION

Although excellent, the D7200's flash metering is not infallible. You may also want to adjust flash levels for creative effect. Flash compensation works with compatible Speedlights or the built-in flash.

To use flash compensation, rotate the sub-command dial while pressing ⚡. It can be set from −3 to +1 Ev in ⅓ Ev steps. After use, reset to zero.

Negative compensation reduces the brightness of flash-lit areas, but has no effect on areas lit by ambient light. Positive compensation brightens areas lit by the flash, again leaving other areas unaffected. However, if the subject is already at the limit of flash range, positive compensation can't help. Instead, use a wider aperture, set a higher ISO, or move closer.

› Manual flash

If Custom setting e3 **Flash cntrl for built-in flash** is set to **Manual**, you can control flash output even more precisely, from **Full** to as low as **1/128**.

› FV lock

FV (flash value) lock is analogous to exposure lock (page 64). When you want to use flash with an off-center subject, you can lock flash output and then reframe the image.

FLASH COMPENSATION ⌄
The base exposure remains the same for these three shots and the background (a daylit garden) looks the same in all three. The foreground, lit by flash, looks quite different with flash compensation settings of −1, 0, and +1.
125mm, 1/320 sec., f/5.6, ISO 100.

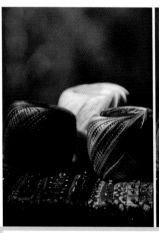
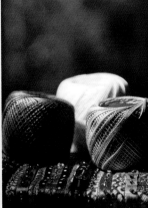
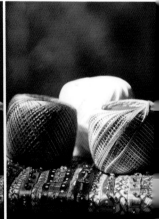

However, it requires a convoluted process, starting by assigning FV lock to the Fn, Preview, or **AE-L/AF-L** button, via Custom Setting f2, f3, or f4 respectively. For occasional use, flash compensation is more convenient.

Having assigned a button to FV lock, the procedure is similar to exposure lock. With the flash charged and ⚡ showing in the viewfinder, position the subject centrally in the frame and half-press the shutter release to activate metering, then press the assigned control button. A pre-flash fires to set the flash level, and FV lock icons appear in the displays. Reframe the image and shoot. The flash level remains locked for succeeding shots; to clear it, press the assigned button again.

› Flash bracketing

Flash bracketing is another way to ensure exactly the right level of flash illumination. It works just like exposure bracketing (page 63). Indeed, you can bracket both flash and main exposure simultaneously. Set Custom Setting e6 **Auto bracketing set** to **Flash only** (to vary flash level only) or **AE & flash** (to vary the main exposure as well).

You then proceed exactly as for exposure bracketing. Use **BKT** and the main command dial to set number of shots in the bracketing burst. **BKT** and the sub-command dial set the difference in flash output between shots.

FLASH PAST ⌄
Here remote flash was used with flash compensation.
16mm, 1/250 sec., f/18, ISO 400.

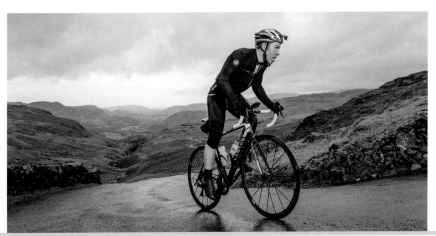

» ACCESSORY FLASHGUNS

Accessory flashguns, which Nikon calls Speedlights, offer much greater power and flexibility than the built-in flash. Nikon Speedlights integrate with Nikon's Creative Lighting System for outstanding results. Independent makers such as Sigma offer alternatives, many also compatible with i-TTL flash control.

NIKON D7200 AND SPEEDLIGHT SB-500 ⩔

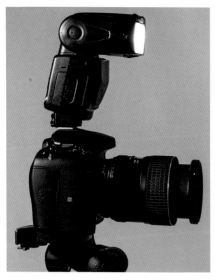

› Using non-Nikon units

Nikon warns against using other brands of flash, and it's true that some flashguns may use too high a trigger voltage or even the wrong polarity, which could damage the camera's circuitry. It's prudent to avoid any non-Nikon flashgun unless it's from a reputable maker such as Sigma or Metz, and their information clearly states that the unit is compatible.

› Mounting an external flashgun

Check the flashgun is switched off and its mounting lock is released. Slide its foot into the camera's hotshoe and lock it in place. Switch on the flashgun. Once it is charged and ready, ⚡ appears in the viewfinder.

> ### Tip
>
> *Flashguns are greedy for battery power. It is always wise to carry at least one set of spares.*

» NIKON CREATIVE LIGHTING SYSTEM

Nikon's Creative Lighting System (CLS), launched in 2003, made flash photography easier and more flexible through innovations including i-TTL flash metering, FV lock, advanced wireless control, and high-speed sync.

CLS requires a compatible camera (like the D7200) and one or more compatible flashguns. These include all current Nikon Speedlights plus several earlier models, listed on page 160; current models are described in more detail.

Many older Nikon flashguns can also be used with the D7200 but advanced CLS functions will not be available. The Nikon manual gives details.

› High-speed flash sync

Nikon's SB-910, SB-700, and SB-R200 Speedlights (and a few older models) offer Auto FP High Speed sync. This phases the flash output, allowing flash to be used at fast shutter speeds. This is useful, for instance, when ambient light levels are high and you wish to use a wide aperture, or when using fill-in flash with fast-moving subjects.

Enable Auto FP High Speed sync using Custom setting e1: set either **1/320s (Auto FP)** or **1/250s (Auto FP)**. With a suitable Speedlight, flash can then be used at any shutter speed from 30 sec. to 1/8000 sec.

However, the effective power (and therefore working range) of the Speedlight does reduce as the shutter speed gets faster. See the individual Speedlight manual for more details, and take test shots if at all possible.

NIKON SPEEDLIGHT SB-500

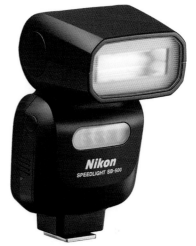

4 » BOUNCE FLASH AND OFF-CAMERA FLASH

Mounting a flashgun in the hotshoe is a start, but its light remains harsh and close to the lens axis, and red-eye remains a common issue. You can dramatically alter the quality of light by bouncing flash off a ceiling, wall, or reflector or by taking the flashgun off the camera entirely.

› Bounce flash

Bouncing the flash light off a suitable surface spreads and softens the light, and changes its direction, allowing more varied and interesting results.

Many flashguns have heads that can be tilted and swiveled so light can easily be bounced off walls, ceilings, and other surfaces. Most surfaces absorb some light, and light also has to travel further; i-TTL metering will automatically compensate, but the working range is reduced. For neutral results choose a white or silvered reflecting surface. Portrait photographers often use gold reflectors for warmer results.

› Off-camera flash

Taking the flash off the camera gives complete control over the direction of light. The flash can be fired wirelessly (see opposite) or using a flash cord; Nikon's dedicated cords preserve i-TTL metering.

FLASH COMPARISON ⌄
The first shot was taken using the built-in flash; there's an ugly shadow yet the subject itself looks flat. The second uses off-camera flash from the left, creating strong modeling. The third uses bounce flash, giving softer, more even light. *100mm macro, f/8, ISO 200.*

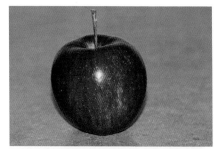

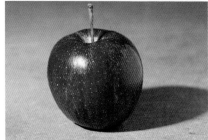

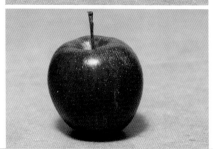

› Wireless flash

CLS-compatible flashguns communicate fully with the camera and its powerful metering system. The D7200's built-in flash can act as "commander", controlling multiple Speedlights in one or two groups. This elevates it from an "amateur" feature to a powerful professional tool.

To enable commander mode use Custom setting e3 **Flash cntrl for built-in flash**. To allow the camera to regulate the output of the remote flashgun(s), set **mode** to **TTL** for each unit or group. **Comp** settings are exactly like flash compensation (page 154).

Radio-control systems offer greater range and allow you to use third-party flashguns. Pocket Wizard systems are well regarded, and I've had excellent results using the less expensive Phottix Odin.

Using multiple flashes in a wireless system gives terrific power and flexibility, but it's not easy to visualize all the possible permutations. It's wise to have a few "dry runs" before an important shoot.

WIRELESS FLASH ⌄
I checked the ambient exposure first, to ensure that the distant scene was well captured. To light the interior of the wreck, I handheld a Nikon Speedlight, to the left and above the camera, using the self-timer to trip the shutter and the camera's own flash as commander.
12mm, 1/60 sec., f/11, ISO 100.

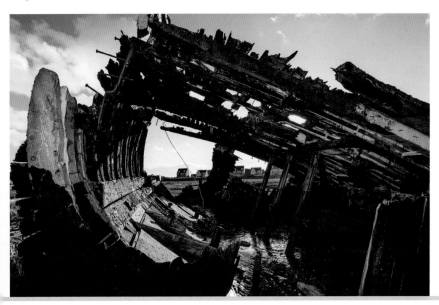

» NIKON SPEEDLIGHTS

DISCONTINUED CLS-COMPATIBLE NIKON SPEEDLIGHTS

	Guide number for ISO 100 (meters)	Use as a commander?	Current or discontinued?
SB-900	34	Yes	Discontinued
SB-800	38	Yes	Discontinued
SB-600	30	No	Discontinued
SB-400	21	No	Discontinued

KEY FEATURES OF CURRENT NIKON SPEEDLIGHTS

	SB-910	SB-700	SB-500	SB-300	SB-R200
Flash coverage (lens focal length range) with D7200	17–200mm	24–120mm	24mm	18mm	
Guide Number (meters, ISO 100)	34	28	24	18	
Tilt/swivel	Yes	Yes	Yes	Tilt only	No
Dimensions (width x height x depth, mm)	78.5 x 145 x 113	71 x 126 x 104.5	67 x 114.55 x 70.8	57.4 x 65.4 x 62.3	80 x 75 x 55
Weight (without batteries)	510g	360g	273g	120g	120g
Use as commander?	Yes	Yes	Yes	No	No (cannot be used in camera hotshoe, only as a slave within Creative Lighting System)

» FLASH ACCESSORIES

Flash accessories such as diffusers, reflectors, and remote leads allow yet more flexibility and control over lighting effects, while power packs increase flash capacity.

Diffusers inevitably reduce the light reaching the subject; flash metering will compensate, but the effective range will be reduced.

› Speedlight Stand AS-19

Allows Speedlights to stand on flat surfaces or mount on a tripod.

› Flash diffusers

Flash diffusers are a simple, economical way to spread and soften the hard light from a flash head. Both the SB-910 and SB-700 include a small dome-type diffuser; larger third-party units like those from Honl give almost a "soft-box" effect.

› Flash brackets

Nikon's Speedlights can be mounted on a tripod or stand on any flat surface using the AS-19 stand, but for more portable support, many photographers prefer a flexible arm or bracket attached to the camera; Novoflex produces a wide range.

D7200 WITH SB-700 AND HONL DIFFUSER ⌄

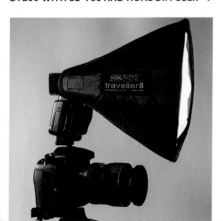

DIFFUSED LIGHT ⌄
Using a setup like that in the previous photo gives light which has a sense of direction but is much softer than using a "naked" Speedlight.
100mm macro, f/11, ISO 100.

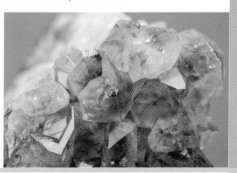

5 CLOSE-UP

Close-up photography is fascinating, but certainly can be challenging. A key issue is depth of field, which becomes ever narrower as distance to the subject shrinks. This often necessitates using small apertures, which can make long exposures essential. Narrow depth of field also means that the slightest movement of either subject or camera can completely ruin focus. A tripod or other solid camera support is often required, and sometimes you'll want to immobilize the subject (within ethical limits).

With minimal depth of field, focusing becomes critical. Rather than merely focusing on the "subject", you must decide which part of the subject—an insect's eye, the stamen of a flower, for instance—to focus on. The 51 AF points cover a good spread, but Live View has much to offer. In Live View you can set the focus point anywhere in the frame, and you can zoom in for greater precision. This also makes manual focus both easy and ultra-precise, and I almost never use AF for macro work.

» MACRO PHOTOGRAPHY

"Close-up" is a vague term, but "macro" has a precise definition; it means photographing subjects at a reproduction ratio of 1:1 or better. Many lenses are badged "macro" when their reproduction ratio is only 1:4, or 1:2 at best. There's still plenty of close-up potential, but it isn't classic macro.

You can explore macro photography without the expense of a dedicated macro lens—see page 166.

RUSTING PIECE »
Most photography is about capturing what you can see with the naked eye. Close-up photography goes beyond this into a whole new world, or at least a new way of seeing the world. *100mm macro, 1/80 sec., f/8, ISO 200, tripod.*

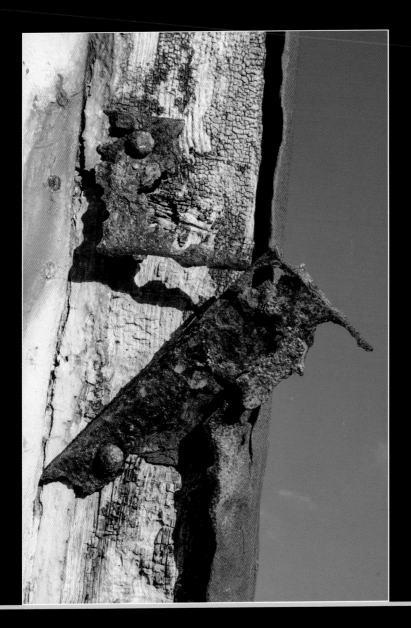

5 » REPRODUCTION RATIO

The reproduction ratio is the ratio between the actual size of the subject and the size of its image on the D7200's DX-format imaging sensor, which measures 23.5 x 15.6mm. At 1:1, an object of this size (smaller than an SD memory card) fills the image exactly. When the image is printed, or displayed on a computer screen, it may appear far larger, but that's another story.

A 1:4 ratio means that a frame-filling subject is four times as long/wide as the sensor, or roughly 3.7 x 2.5 inches (approximately 94 x 62mm)—slightly larger than a credit card.

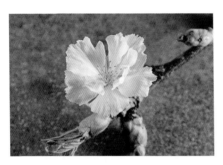

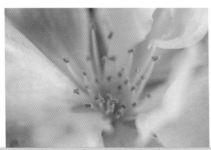

› Working distance

This is the distance required for a given reproduction ratio with a specific lens. It relates directly to focal length: a 200mm lens doubles the working distance for the same reproduction ratio compared to a 100mm. Extra distance can help when photographing mobile subjects and ones which might be damaged by accidental contact. It also makes it easier to get good light onto the subject.

It is measured from the focal plane, effectively the surface of the sensor. A 9in. (25cm) working distance can put the subject less than 4in. (10cm) from the front of the lens. Lens hoods or ring-flash can narrow this even more.

> **Tip**
>
> *1.3x crop offers a handy way to increase effective working distance— and if you're using autofocus it also means that the focus points cover most of the image area.*

READY FOR THE CLOSE-UP «
The first shot has a reproduction ratio of approximately 1:4. The second, taken with a macro lens at minimum distance, gives approximately life size (1:1) reproduction.
85mm/100mm macro, 1/80 sec., f/8, ISO 200.

» MACRO LIGHTING

The built-in flash activates automatically in 🌷 Close up mode, yet it's practically useless for real macro photography, as the lens blocks its light with really close subjects. Shadows—your own, or the camera's—often intrude when you're using available light, too. With macro subjects, it's often crucial, but can be tricky, to direct the light exactly where it's needed.

Ring-flash units encircle the lens, giving even illumination on ultra-close subjects (they're also favored by some portrait photographers). They are available from Sigma, Nissin, and others.

Nikon prefers a twin-flash approach with its Speedlight Commander Kit R1C1 and

Speedlight Remote Kit R1. Both use Speedlight SB-R200 flashguns, mounting either side of the lens. The R1C1 includes a Wireless Speedlight Commander SU-800, which fits into the camera's hotshoe, while the R1 needs a separate commander. Either way, it's an expensive package.

› LED light

LED lights, like the Sunpak DSLR67 LED Macro Ring Light, are much cheaper. It's only suitable for close subjects, but that's all you need in a macro light. You may still need fairly high ISO ratings to achieve fast shutter speeds for mobile subjects.

RING LIGHT ⌄
D7200 and Sunpak LED Macro Ring Light (this is an older version, not the DSLR67).

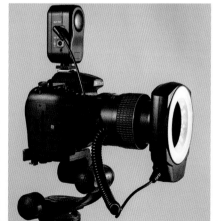

LED LIGHT ⌄
This image was taken with the Sunpak LED Macro Ring Light (left).
100mm macro, 1 sec., f/11, ISO 100, tripod.

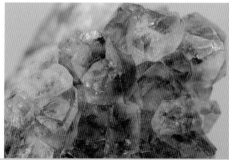

5 » EQUIPMENT FOR MACRO PHOTOGRAPHY

Close-up attachment lenses are simple magnifying lenses that screw into the filter thread of the lens. They are light, inexpensive, and fully compatible with the camera's exposure and focusing systems. Results are generally best in conjunction with prime lenses. Nikon produces six close-up attachment lenses (see table below).

› Extension tubes

Extension tubes, or extension rings, are another simple, economical, way to extend a lens' close-focusing capabilities. The tubes, mounting between the lens and the camera, decrease the minimum focusing distance, and increase the magnification factor. They are light, compact, and easy to carry and attach.

Nikon produces four extension rings, but all are an elderly design and inordinately expensive. A set of three compatible tubes (12mm, 20mm, and 36mm) from Kenko costs little more than a single Nikon tube. They fully support metering and auto-exposure. They don't support autofocus with all lenses, but that's a minor issue in most macro work.

> **Warning!**
>
> **Some lenses are incompatible with accessories like extension tubes and bellows. Check the lens' manual.**

› Bellows

Like extension tubes, bellows extend the spacing between the lens and the camera body, but offer a greater range of extension. However, they are expensive, heavy, and slow to set up—they are for the experienced macro specialist only.

› Reversing rings

Also known as reverse adapters or inversion rings, these allow lenses to be mounted in reverse, allowing them to focus much closer than when used normally. They are ideally used with a prime lens. Nikon's Inversion ring BR-2A fits a 52mm filter thread.

PRODUCT NUMBER	ATTACHES TO FILTER THREAD	RECOMMENDED FOR USE WITH
0, 1	52mm	Standard lenses
3T, 4T	52mm	Short telephoto lenses
5T, 6T	62mm	Telephoto lenses

CAREFUL FOCUS   ≫

At 1:1 or higher reproduction ratios, depth of field can be minuscule and careful focusing on an exact point of your subject is essential.
100mm macro, 1/200 sec., f/5.6, ISO 100, tripod.

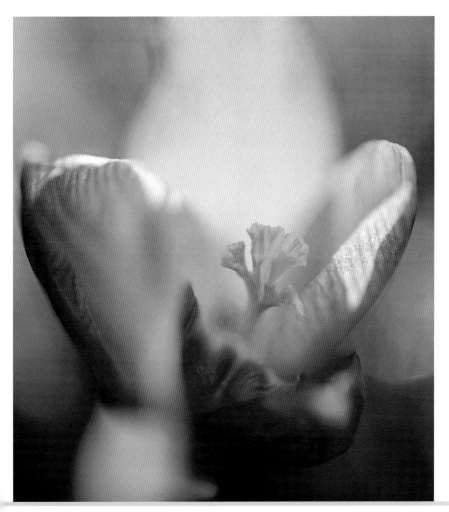

5 » MACRO LENSES

True macro lenses give reproduction ratios of 1:1 or better and are optically optimized for close-up work, though very capable for general photography too. This is certainly true of Nikon's Micro Nikkor lenses. Of course, other makers also produce excellent macro lenses: the lens used for all the close-up images in this book is a 100mm Tokina.

› DX macro lenses

Two of Nikon's macro lenses are specifically designed for the DX format.

The **40mm f/2.8G AF-S DX Micro Nikkor** is Nikon's lightest, and least expensive, macro lens, and works well as a standard lens too. However, its working distance at 1:1 reproduction ratio is just 6in. (or 16cm), leaving very little room between the subject and the front of the lens.

The **85mm f/3.5G ED VR AF-S DX Micro Nikkor** also achieves 1:1 reproduction—with approximately double the working distance—and has VRII, internal focusing, as well as ED glass.

› FX macro lenses

Nikon's full-frame macro lenses work equally well on the D7200.

The **60mm f/2.8G ED AF-S Micro Nikkor** has ED glass for superior optical quality and Silent Wave Motor for ultra-quiet autofocus.

The **105mm f/2.8G AF-S VR Micro Nikkor** was the world's first macro lens with VR (Vibration Reduction). It also features internal focusing, ED glass, and Silent Wave Motor.

The **200mm f/4D ED-IF AF Micro Nikkor** is an older design, but its longer working distance makes it particularly suited to photographing the animal kingdom.

40MM F/2.8G AF-S DX MICRO NIKKOR ❯❯

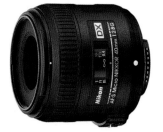

85MM F/3.5G ED VR AF-S DX MICRO NIKKOR ❯❯

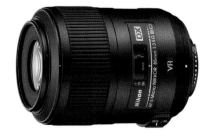

› Vibration Reduction

As the slightest camera shake is magnified at high reproduction ratios, VR (Vibration Reduction) technology seems like a very good thing, allowing you to employ shutter speeds—in theory at least—up to four stops slower than otherwise possible. However, VR only allows for movement of the camera; it can't compensate for movement of the subject.

It's also almost impossible to avoid swaying slightly when handholding, and at close range the slightest change in subject-to-camera distance can completely ruin the focus. In macro shooting, VR is no substitute for care and a good tripod.

VIOLET   ❮
Violets are highly mobile in even the slightest breeze. Vibration reduction is no use at all in countering this. Pick a perfectly calm day or find some way of shielding them.
100mm macro, 1/60 sec., f/11, ISO 100, tripod.

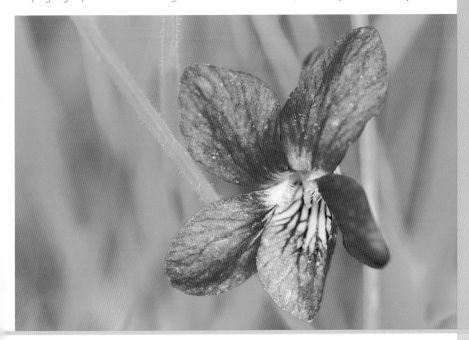

6 MOVIES

For many, the true purpose of the DSLR is to shoot stills, and its ergonomics are still best for this. However, video is no mere sideshow. Many movie makers have embraced DSLRs because their large sensors deliver image quality that's superior—and just plain different—to standard camcorders, while photojournalists welcome the ability to shoot high-quality stills and video on the same camera. However, movies and still photography are very different, requiring distinctly different approaches for best results.

» ADVANTAGES

DSLRs in general, not least the D7200, have some real advantages over standard camcorders. The large sensor allows much shallower depth of field; movie-makers have eagerly embraced this "DSLR look". DSLRs also offer greater dynamic range, and better quality at high ISO ratings, extending the possibilities for low-light shooting.

Another plus is compatibility with the array of Nikon-fit lenses (see Chapter 7): in particular, the D7200 can use wide-angle lenses which exceed the range of most camcorders.

Camcorders often claim enormous zoom ranges, but beware of "digital zoom", a software function that merely enlarges the central portion of the image.

"Optical zoom" range is what matters, and interchangeable lenses cover all normal angles of view. The widest range currently available in a single Nikon lens is 18–300mm. Tamron produces a 16–300mm.

THE "DSLR LOOK" »
It's much easier to get really shallow depth of field than with most video cameras—especially using a 50mm lens at close range with an aperture of f/1.8.

WIDE AND HANDSOME »
A 12mm focal length gives a very wide and dramatic view.

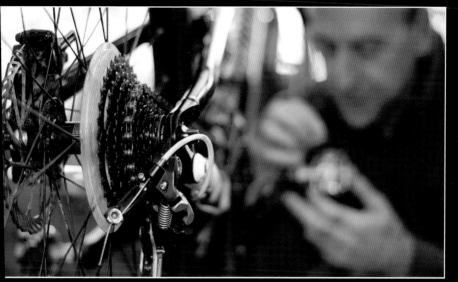

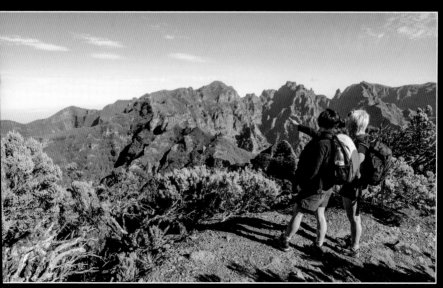

6 » MAKING MOVIES

› Preparation

Make sure that the Lv Live View selector is set to 🎥.

Before shooting, select key settings in the Movie Shooting menu (see opposite). You can also access many of these from Movie Live View by pressing ◀🔲 to reveal a list at the right side of the screen (see the second column in the table opposite). This is just like using Live View quick settings (page 91), although the options are different. Only a few of these can be accessed while actually shooting.

The available options include familiar ones like Picture Controls and white balance, which must be set appropriately (if using P, S, A, or M exposure modes). You can check the general look of a shot by taking a still frame from Movie Live View before starting movie recording.

The limited availability of "on the fly" exposure options may be a blessing in disguise. Executing any of these operations while actually shooting is fiddly. It's difficult to avoid jogging the camera, unless it's on a solid tripod, and they also produce extraneous sounds, to which the built-in microphone is all-too-sensitive. Another consequence could be jarring changes in brightness midway through a shot. It's best to get the settings right beforehand and then just leave well alone.

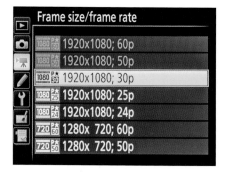

SETTING FRAME SIZE/FRAME RATE IN ⊗
THE MOVIE SETTINGS SECTION OF THE
PHOTO SHOOTING MENU

Other options are specific to movie shooting.

Frame size/frame rate sets the movie image size and frame rate. The size options are **1920 x 1080** pixels and **1280 x 720** pixels. The available frame rate options vary according to the size chosen.

60p and **50p** frame rate options are only available when Image area is set to **1.3x crop** (see page 174). These higher frame rates can give a half-speed slow-motion effect when played back, or can give a slightly smoother appearance to action.

Movie quality sets the compression level; options are **High** or **Normal**. Footage recorded to a memory card is always compressed to some degree, though High

ACCESS TO MOVIE SETTINGS

Movie Shooting menu	Movie Quick Settings	Notes
Reset Movie Shooting menu		
File naming		
Destination	Destination	
Frame size/frame rate	Frame size/frame rate	
Movie quality	Movie quality	
Microphone sensitivity	Microphone sensitivity	
Frequency response	Frequency response	
Wind noise reduction	Wind noise reduction	
Image area	Image area	
White balance	White balance	Can also be set with **WB** and main command dial
Set Picture Control	Set Picture Control	
Manage Picture Control		
High ISO NR		
Movie ISO sensitivity settings		Sensitivity (mode M) can be set with **ISO** and main command dial
Time-lapse photography		
	Monitor brightness	
	Highlight display	
	Headphone volume	

quality is fine for most purposes (akin to JPEG Fine for stills). However, the D7200 can export uncompressed footage when a compatible recorder is connected to the camera's HDMI port.

Microphone sensitivity applies either to the built-in microphone or an external one if attached. The options are: **Auto**, **Manual Sensitivity** (in steps from 1-20), and **Off**. You can see an audio-level display while in this menu, making it easy to do a "soundcheck".

Frequency response and **Wind noise reduction** also both relate to sound quality. The Frequency response options are **Wide range** or **Vocal range**. Vocal range can give clearer results when recording dialog but can give poor results when recording other sounds (e.g. birdsong). Wind noise reduction applies only to the built-in microphones. Enabling it can indeed reduce the level of wind noise but may also impair the quality of other sound. The best way to reduce wind noise is to use an external microphone.

Image area

The D7200 records movies with a "widescreen" aspect ratio of 16:9; normally these use the full width of the sensor. You can also select **1.3x crop**; the camera then employs a smaller area, giving a "teleconverter" effect (page 196). The screen automatically shows the area which is being used. This does not affect the

output size of the footage; you can still record 1920 x 1080 as well as 1280 x 720.

Movie ISO sensitivity settings

ISO options in movie shooting are very limited. In fact, except in mode M, ISO control is automatic, though you can set an upper limit as you do for Auto ISO sensitivity control in stills.

To set ISO manually in Manual mode, set **Auto ISO control (mode M)** to **Off**.

Monitor brightness

Allows adjustment of screen brightness. As with regular Live View, remember that this does not change the actual exposure level of footage you shoot.

Highlight display

Enable/disable the Highlight display for exposure judgement.

Headphone volume

Self-explanatory, and only relevant if using external headphones.

› Focus options

The focus modes and AF-area options for movie shooting are the same as for Live View (page 92). In Full-time servo AF (AF-F), the D7200 will automatically maintain focus during movie recording, though Live View AF is nowhere near agile enough for fast-moving subjects. It's important to be aware of this limitation. Sometimes you just have to work round it and plan alternative shots that don't stress the AF system so far.

In Single-servo AF (AF-S) the camera will only refocus when you half-press the shutter-release button.

Manual focusing is also possible, but can be yet another recipe for wobbly pictures. A tripod helps, especially with longer lenses, where focusing is more critical and wobbles are magnified. Some lenses have a smoother manual focus action than others. Older lenses often have large, well-placed focus rings. There are attachments (often expensive!) which allow you to control focus more smoothly and precisely.

Unexpected or inaccurate focus shifts can be very disconcerting when viewing the footage. Fortunately, fixed focus is perfectly viable for many shots, especially when depth of field is good. To employ fixed focus, use AF-S (Single-servo AF), set focus in Live View before shooting the clip, and avoid pressing the shutter-release button while shooting. Or just use manual focus.

› Exposure

In Program or Shutter-priority mode, exposure levels can be adjusted by ±3 Ev using 🔲 and the main command dial. Shutter speed, aperture, and ISO are set automatically. The only other exposure-related option you can change is the metering pattern (center-weighted or matrix

only). In fact, for movies there is no functional difference between P and S modes. Scene modes have similar options (or lack of them), except that you can't change the metering pattern. In Full Auto and Effects modes exposure is entirely automatic.

More extensive exposure control is only available in A and M modes. In Aperture-priority mode, aperture can be manually adjusted, but only by exiting Live View. Aperture control is vital if you're seeking to create "DSLR-look" footage with slender depth of field. Shutter speed and ISO are set automatically.

Manual mode allows direct control over shutter speed and ISO sensitivity. However, allowing auto-ISO means that the camera can accommodate changes in light level on the fly; making manual adjustments may create noise or camera shake, and may also lag behind light levels.

Shutter speed does affect how moving subjects are recorded, so can be very important. However, the available shutter speed range is limited (see the next page). Again, aperture can only be adjusted by exiting Live View.

> ### Tip
>
> *To avoid sudden changes in brightness in your footage, you can lock exposure by holding* **AE-L/AF-L** *just as in stills photography.*

You can (in good light) set shutter speeds right up to 1/4000 sec., but there are inescapable limits to the slowest speed you can select. For instance, if frame rate is 24 or 25, the slowest possible speed is 1/25 sec.—you obviously can't shoot 25 x 1/2 sec. exposures in one second! Similarly, the slowest possible shutter speed at 50p is 1/50 sec., and 1/60 sec. for 60p.

Still photography experience suggests that faster shutter speeds give sharper pictures. Movies work differently. If you shoot at 1/500 sec., while each frame may appear sharp if examined individually, the clip often appears jerky when played. This is because each second contains 25 discrete slices of action (assuming 25p frame rate). 25 times 1/500 sec. is just 5% of the action. The nearer the shutter speed is to 1/25 sec., the nearer you get to capturing 100%, and the smoother the motion appears on playback.

However, in bright conditions, you can't shoot at 1/30 sec. and simultaneously use a really wide aperture for shallow depth of field, even at ISO 100—except by employing a neutral density filter.

SLOW TRAIN ⌄
A slow shutter speed helps to render movement more smoothly.
18mm, 1/50 sec., f/16, ISO 100.

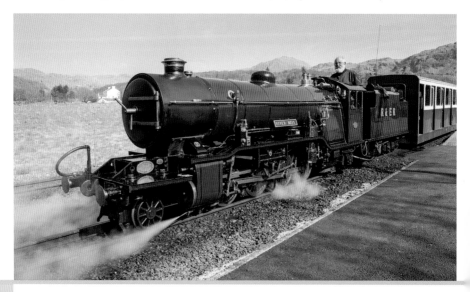

> ## Highlight display

Most of the usual methods of judging exposure are available in Movie Live View—and the D7200 has an extra trick up its sleeve, specifically for movies. If you press ◂⬛▸ in Movie Live View and select **Highlight display>On**, the camera will display diagonal "zebra stripes" in areas which may be blown out or "clipped" (see page 99).

> ## Sound

The D7200's built-in microphone gives reasonable quality stereo output. However, it's all too good at picking up any sounds you make operating the camera (focusing, zooming, even breathing). If you want to include dialog or "talking heads", keep subjects close to the camera and ensure that background noise is minimized.

Fortunately, the D7200 also lets you connect an external microphone to the 3.5mm socket under the cover on the camera's left side. This automatically overrides the internal microphone.

The D7200 lets you monitor sound during shooting by plugging headphones into the appropriate socket. You can adjust recording level while shooting, provided you've selected **Manual Sensitivity** in the **Microphone sensitivity** section of the Movie Shooting menu beforehand.

> ## Shooting

1) Choose exposure mode. Set aperture if using A or M mode.

2) Set ⬛Lv⬛ to the 🎥 position and activate Movie Live View by pressing its center-button. Check AF mode and AF-area mode. Select other options as required from the Movie Shooting menu and/or by pressing ◂⬛▸.

3) Check framing and exposure. Initialize focus by half-pressure on the shutter release (or focus manually).

4) Check sound levels.

5) Press ⊙ to start recording the movie. **REC** flashes red at the top of the screen while recording, and an indicator shows the maximum remaining shooting time.

6) To stop recording, press ⊙ again.

7) Exit Live View by pressing ⬛Lv⬛.

> ### Tip

You can also use the shutter-release button to start and end movie recording: see Custom Setting g4 **Assign shutter button**. *This removes the option to shoot a still frame directly during movie recording.*

Plan ahead. If a still image isn't perfect, you can review it, change position or settings, and be ready to reshoot within seconds. To shoot and review even a short movie clip eats up much more time, and you may not get a second chance anyway. It's doubly important to get shooting position, framing, and camera settings right beforehand. You can check the general look of the shot by shooting a still frame, but this does not allow for movement of subject, camera, or both; you can also do a dry run in Live View.

If you're new to movies, start with simple shots. Don't try zooming, panning, and focusing simultaneously: do one at a time. Many subjects can be filmed with a fixed camera: waterfalls, musicians playing, and

loads more. Practice panning and zooming on relatively static subjects like landscapes too.

› Handling

It's impossible to overstress the importance of a tripod for shooting decent movies. VR lens technology can counteract short-frequency shake, but does nothing to eliminate slower (and often larger) wobbles. Of course even "real" movie

ACROSS THE WATER ☙
Panning with the boat is an obvious shot, but the tripod needs to be leveled correctly, or the water could start to develop a steep slope!

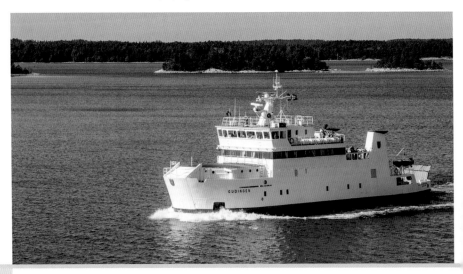

directors sometimes use handheld cameras to create a specific feel, but in a controlled way and for deliberate effect.

Using a tripod, or other suitable camera support, is the simplest way to give movie clips a polished, professional look. If one isn't available, look for other alternatives. A beanbag is great for static shots. If you have to handhold, try to brace your elbows on your knees or on a solid surface.

A standard tripod with a pan-and-tilt head is fine to start with. For best results, especially when panning, dedicated video tripods (or tripod heads) are specifically designed to move smoothly.

When a tripod isn't practicable, there are many accessory grips and stabilizers to improve handling and stability, including smaller versions of the legendary Steadicam used by professional cameramen.

› Panning

The panning shot is a staple, whether for following moving subjects, or giving a dynamic view of static ones; for instance, sweeping across a panorama.

Handheld panning is problematic; it may be acceptable when following a

MOUNTAIN BIKING　⌄
A classic panning shot, but not easy to follow neatly when the rider is moving at speed.

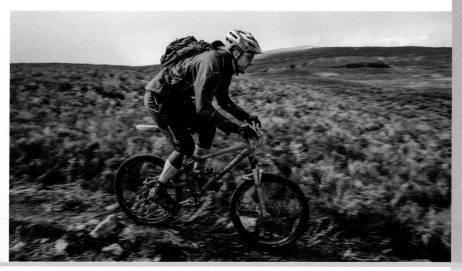

moving subject, but a wobbly pan across a grand landscape grates badly. Nothing really replaces a tripod for this. Make sure it's properly leveled, too.

Panning too rapidly can make the shot hard to "read" and even nauseate the viewer. Smooth panning is easiest with video tripods. In any case, a bit of practice pays dividends.

With moving subjects, the speed and direction of panning is dictated by the need to keep the subject in frame. Accurate tracking of fast-moving subjects is very challenging and takes a lot of practice.

› Zooming

The zoom is another fundamental technique. Moving from a wide view to a tighter one is zooming in, the converse zooming out. As ever, forward planning makes all the difference; consider how the shot will look at both extremes. When zooming in to a specific subject, check it's central in frame.

EXPLORING
The camera can "explore" a scene like this either by panning across it or by zooming in on specific aspects of the landscape.

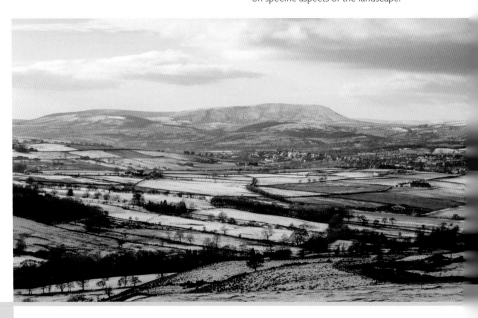

Available lenses lack the extreme zoom range of some camcorder lenses but, more seriously, it's hard to achieve a really smooth, even-paced zoom action. Practice helps; mounting the camera on a solid tripod helps even more. Powered zoom would be a real help, but no current DSLR lenses offer this feature. Nikon already makes power-zoom lenses for its Nikon 1 mirrorless cameras, so who knows what may be in store?

When zooming, remember that depth of field decreases toward the telephoto end of the range. Your subject may appear perfectly sharp in a wide-angle view but end up looking soft when you zoom in. Preset focus at the telephoto end of the range.

› Lighting

For obvious reasons, you can't use flash; lighting must be continuous. There are now many LED light units specifically designed for DSLR-movie shooting. The D7200's ability to maintain decent quality at high ISO ratings is also invaluable.

› Still frame capture

To capture a still frame during movie shooting, simply press the shutter-release button. This will end movie recording, take the shot, and return you to Live View. The resulting image will use the 16:9 aspect ratio; quality and size are determined by your still-image settings. For image sizes, see the table below.

You can also extract a still frame from an existing movie clip, but don't expect miracles. The image size will be the same as your selected movie frame size (1920 x 1080 or 1280 x 720 pixels) and motion which appears smooth when playing the movie may well look blurred in the single frame.

Image area	Image size setting	Size in pixels
DX movie	Large (or RAW)	6000 x 3368
	Medium	4496 x 2528
	Small	2992 x 1680
1.3x crop	Large (or RAW)	4800 x 2696
	Medium	3600 x 2024
	Small	2400 x 1344

6 » EDITING

The D7200 doesn't shoot movies. Like all movie cameras, it shoots movie clips. Turning a collection of clips into a movie that people actually want to see generally requires editing, and usually Non-Linear Editing. This simply means that clips in the final movie don't have to appear in the same order in which they were shot. Digital editing is also non-destructive; unlike cutting and splicing bits of film, it doesn't affect your original footage. During editing, you manipulate preview versions of your clips and the software merely keeps "notes" on the edit. At the end, you export the result as a new movie, while all the original clips remain intact.

› Software

Nikon now offers movie editing software for Mac and Windows as part of the View NXi suite. ViewNX Movie Editor is a basic editing package but handles all the key tasks.

More sophisticated options are also available at no cost. Mac users have iMovie, part of the iLife suite, included with all new Macs. The Windows equivalent is Windows Movie Maker, a free download from windowslive.com. A more advanced (but not free) option, for either platform, is Adobe Premiere Elements.

All these apps make it easy to trim and reorder your original clips. Instead of simply cutting instantaneously between shots, you can apply transitions such as dissolves, wipes, and fades. You can also adjust the look of any clip or segment of the movie; as well as basic controls for brightness, color, and so on ("grading"), you can add a range of special effects; for instance, making your movie look scratched and faded, as if shot on film 50 years ago rather than yesterday with a DSLR.

You can add other media, like still photographs. You can insert stills individually at appropriate points or create slide shows within the main movie. Again, effects and transitions can be applied to give slide shows a more dynamic feel.

It's equally easy to add a new soundtrack, like a voiceover or music, to part or all of the movie. Last but not least, you can also add titles and captions.

Tip

Effects and transitions are great fun— and non-destructive editing lets you experiment to your heart's content— but, for the audience's sake, keep to a small selection in the final version. Unless you've created them yourself, still photos, music, and other media are someone else's copyright. Look for open-source material or get the copyright owner's permission to use their work.

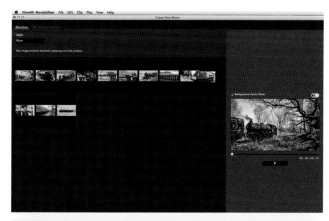

NIKON MOVIE 《
EDITOR

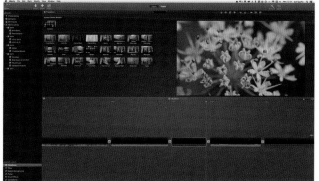

iMOVIE 《

› Taking it further

There's far more to movie-making than we can cover in a single chapter. A useful next step would be *Understanding HD Video* by Chiz Dakin, from this publisher.

7 LENSES

One of the (many) benefits of a DSLR like the D7200 is its ability to use a vast range of lenses, including Nikon's own legendary system as well as lenses from other makers. The Nikon F lens mount was introduced in 1959. It has developed significantly, but most Nikkor lenses will still mount happily on the D7200.

» USING OLDER LENSES

Modern lenses with the suffix E, D, or G provide full functionality with the D7200. Other Nikon lenses with a built-in CPU, designated AF-I or AF-S, will support almost the same range of functions—in practice, you may rarely notice a difference. Check carefully when considering lenses from independent makers (for instance, with Sigma lenses, look for the "HSM" tag).

Older lenses without a built-in CPU, such as AI and AI-S types, can be attached, but will require manual focusing. You'll need to use exposure mode A or M. To use matrix metering with these lenses, enter key data under Non-CPU lens data in the Setup menu.

Very early "non-AI" lenses should not be used—unless modified—as they can damage the camera. A few other (rare) lenses should also be avoided—see the Nikon manual.

CANAL BOAT »
A long (300mm) lens can isolate a few elements of a landscape.
300mm, 1/2500 sec., f/9, ISO 400.

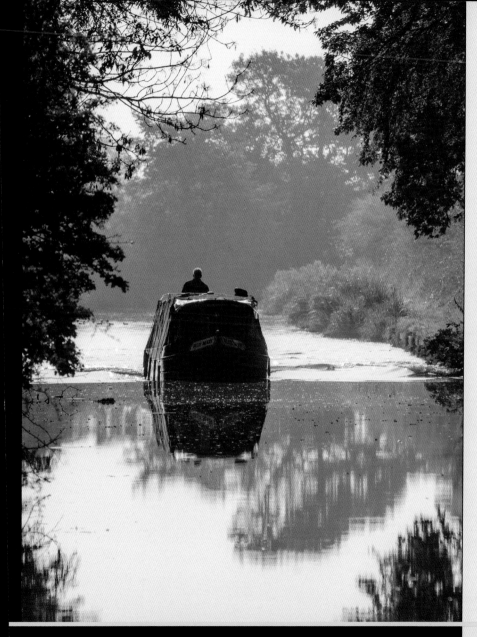

7 » FOCAL LENGTH

Though familiar, the term "focal length" is often used in confusing or misleading ways.

The focal length of any lens is a basic optical characteristic. It is not changed by fitting the lens to a different camera. A 20mm lens is a 20mm lens, no matter what.

However, what is often called the "effective" or "equivalent" focal length can and does change. I can fit the same lenses to the D7200 or to my full-frame (FX) D600, but the results are different because the D600's larger sensor "sees" more of the image that the lens projects.

Another way of expressing this is to say that the field or angle of view of the FX camera is wider. The angle of view can give another way of comparing lenses. It is usually measured on the diagonal of the frame (as in the table on page 200).

FX/DX IMAGE AREA ⌄

The original was shot with a 14mm lens on a full-frame Nikon D750. The red rectangle shows the area that would be captured using the same lens, from the same position, on a DX camera like the D7200.
14mm, 1/80 sec., f/11, ISO 200, tripod.

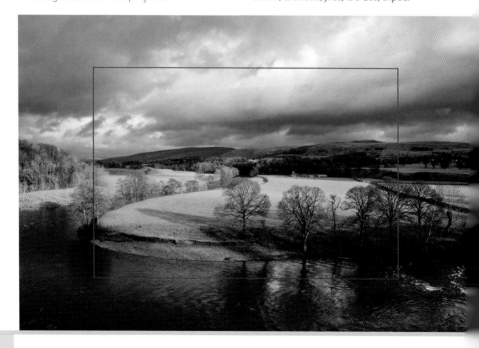

› Crop factor

The D7200's smaller sensor, relative to the 35mm/FX standard, gives it a crop factor, or focal length magnification factor, of 1.5. If you fit a 200mm lens to a D7200, the field of view equates to what you'd see with a 300mm lens on a full-frame camera (e.g. D4 or D600). For sports and wildlife this can be an advantage, allowing long-range shooting with relatively light and inexpensive lenses (and you can crop even more using the 1.3x Image area).

Conversely, the crop factor makes wide-angle lenses effectively less wide, which is unwelcome news for landscape shooters. However, this has fostered the development of new ultra-wide lenses, like the 10–24mm f/3.5–4.5G DX Nikkor.

Nikon's DX lenses are specifically designed for use with DX cameras like the D7200. They can be used on FX cameras, but won't cover the full image area of the larger sensor. DX lenses tend to be smaller and lighter than FX lenses of the same focal length. They are listed first in the table of Nikkor lenses on page 200.

The next page shows a series of images taken on a Nikon D7200, from a fixed position, with a range of lenses from 12mm to 300mm.

Tip

Lenses on digital compact cameras are normally labeled not with their actual focal length but by their "35mm equivalent"; i.e. the focal length that would give the same angle of view on a 35mm or full-frame camera. Throughout this book, and specifically in the shooting details for the photos, the true focal length is used.

7

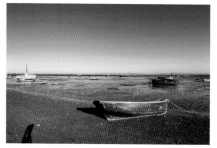

12mm

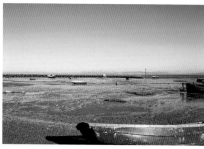

24mm

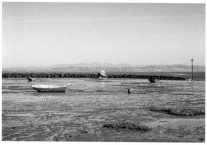

50mm

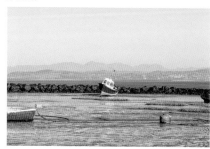

100mm

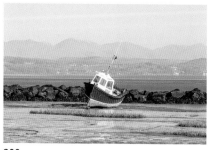

200mm

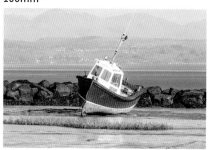

300mm

FOCAL LENGTH COMPARISON ⌃

Each of these photographs was taken with the
Nikon D7200 and a different lens as shown.
1/100 sec., f/11, ISO 100.

» LENS ISSUES

› Flare

Lens flare is usually seen when shooting towards the sun or other bright light sources; caused by reflections within the lens, it may produce a string of colored blobs or a more general misty "veil" effect.

Advanced lens coatings help reduce flare, as does keeping lenses and filters clean. Even so, when the sun's directly in shot, some flare may be inescapable. You can sometimes mask the sun, perhaps behind a tree.

If the sun isn't actually in shot, you can shield the lens. A good lens hood is essential, but may need to be supplemented with a piece of card, a map, or your hand. This is easy when using a tripod; otherwise it requires assistance, or one-handed shooting. Check carefully to see if the flare has gone—and that the shading object hasn't crept into shot.

ELIMINATING FLARE ⌄
The flare in the bottom center is very distracting. A slight change of position and a tighter zoom eliminated it (see page 230).
40mm, 1/400 sec., f/11, ISO 200.

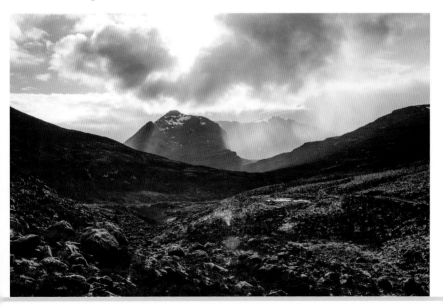

› Distortion

Distortion makes lines which are really straight appear curved in the image. Distortion is usually worst with zoom lenses, especially at the extremes of the zoom range. When straight lines bow outwards, it's called barrel distortion; when they bend inwards it's pincushion distortion. Distortion often goes unnoticed when shooting natural subjects with no straight lines, but can still rear its ugly head when level horizons appear in landscape or seascape images.

Distortion can be corrected using **Auto Distortion Control** in the Photo Shooting menu) (for compatible lenses) or rectified later, using **Distortion Control** in the Retouch menu or in post-processing. However, all these methods crop the image.

› Chromatic aberration

Chromatic aberration occurs when light of different colors is focused in slightly different places on the sensor, and appears as colored fringing when images are examined closely. There is some built-in correction during processing of JPEG images. Aberration can also be corrected in post-processing; with RAW images this is the only option.

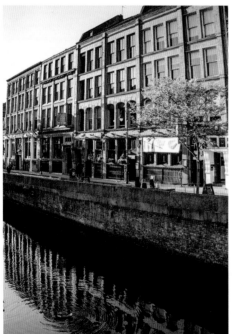

DISTORTION «
Distortion was exaggerated in post-processing—it's hard to spot in the center of the frame, but all too obvious near the edges.
21mm, 1/80 sec., f/9, ISO 200.

› Vignetting

Vignetting is a darkening towards the corners of the image, most conspicuous in even-toned areas such as clear skies. Many lenses show slight vignetting at maximum aperture, but it should reduce on stopping down. There is built-in Vignette control for JPEG images (page 108). It can also be tackled in post-processing.

Severe vignetting can arise if you use unsuitable lens hoods and filter holders, or "stack" multiple filters on the lens.

VIGNETTE ⌄
A strong vignette effect was added in post-processing.
38mm, 1/80 sec., f/11, ISO 200.

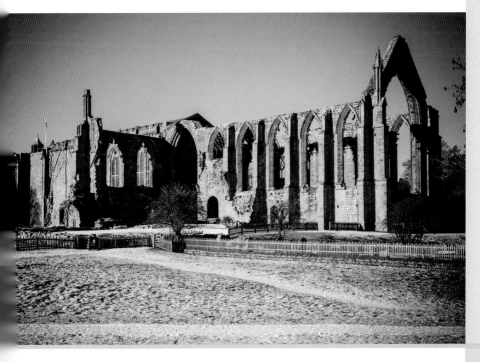

7 » LENS CARE

Lenses require special care. Dust, dirt, and scratches will all degrade your images. Remove dust with a blower. Fingerprints and other marks should only be tackled with a dedicated lens cleaner and optical-grade cloth. Skylight or UV filters (page 208) can protect the lens, and lens caps should be replaced when the lens is not in use.

LENS PROTECTION ⌄
The bulbous front element of this Sigma 12–24mm lens requires extra protection—the lens hood is permanently fixed.

› Lens hoods

A lens hood helps to exclude stray light which may degrade the image and cause flare. It can also shield the lens against knocks, rain, and other hazards. Most Nikkor lenses are supplied with a dedicated hood. Lens hoods are also available separately, but Nikon's own tend to be disproportionately expensive; third-party alternatives can be far cheaper. However, do check that the hood in question is compatible with the lens—try before you buy, taking test shots to check there's no vignetting.

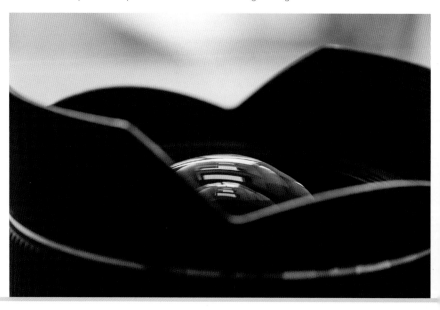

» STANDARD LENSES

In 35mm film photography and full-frame digital, a 50mm lens is called standard, as its field of view is held to approximate that of the human eye; this is debatable, but the label has stuck. Because of the crop factor of the D7200, the equivalent lens is around 35mm. Standard lenses are typically light, simple, and have wide maximum apertures. Zoom lenses whose range includes this focal length are often referred to as "standard zooms".

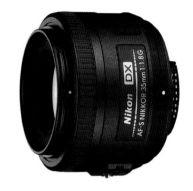

35MM F/1.8G AF–S DX NIKKOR ⨂

COTTAGE RUINS ⨂
Standard lenses are useful in many situations.
35mm, 1/125 sec., f/13, ISO 200.

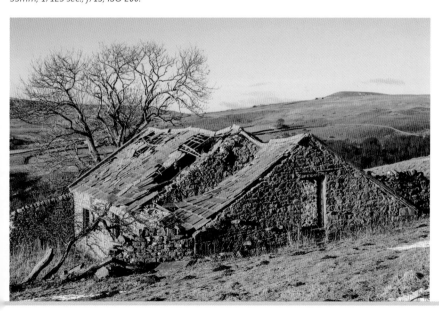

7 » WIDE-ANGLE LENSES

A wide-angle lens is really any lens wider than a standard lens; for the D7200 this means any lens shorter than 35mm. Wide-angle lenses are valuable for working close to subjects or bringing foregrounds into greater prominence. They lend themselves both to photographing expansive scenic views and to working in cramped spaces where you can't step back to "get more in".

Because of the D7200's crop factor, a lens like a 17mm, once regarded as "super-wide", gives a less extreme angle of view. This has promoted the development of a new breed of even wider lenses, including Nikon's 10–24mm and Sigma's 10–20mm offerings.

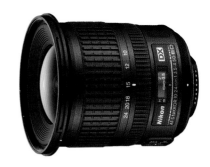

10–24MM F/3.5–4.5G DX NIKKOR ⌃

ABANDONED BOAT ⌄
Wide-angle lenses are perfect for portraying subjects in their environment.
12mm, 1/20 sec., f/11, ISO 100, tripod.

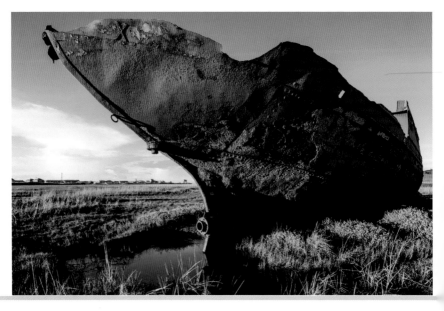

» TELEPHOTO LENSES

Telephoto lenses, often simply called long lenses, give a narrow angle of view. They are closely associated with wildlife and sports photography, but have many other uses, such as singling out small or distant elements in a landscape. Moderate telephoto lenses (around 60–90mm with the D7200) are favored for portrait photography, because the greater working distance gives a natural-looking result and is more comfortable for nervous subjects.

When using telephoto lenses, depth of field tends to be narrow. This is often welcome in portraiture, wildlife, and sport photography, as it concentrates attention on the subject by throwing backgrounds out of focus.

Longer lenses can be heavy, bulky, and hard to handhold comfortably. Their

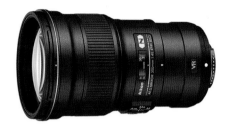

300MM F/4E PF ED VR AF-S NIKKOR ☆

narrow view also magnifies any shake or wobble. High shutter speeds and/or tripods or other camera support are often required. Nikon's Vibration Reduction (VR) technology also mitigates the effects of camera shake, but can slow down the maximum frame rate, which sports shooters in particular need to recognize.

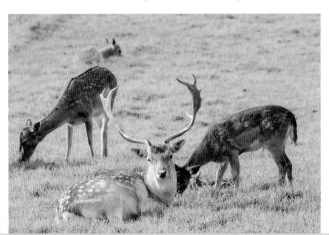

FALLOW DEER «
Telephoto lenses are useful for shooting subjects, such as wildlife, that would be impossible to approach closely. *300mm, 1/400 sec., f/10, ISO 400.*

7 » TELECONVERTERS

Teleconverters are supplementary units which fit between the main lens and the camera body, and magnify the focal length of the main lens. Nikon currently offers the TC-14E III (1.4x magnification), TC-17E II (1.7x), and TC-20E III (2x). The advantages are obvious, extending the focal length with minimal additional weight (the TC-14E III, for example, weighs just 200 grams). Some lenses are incompatible with teleconverters. Check carefully before buying or using one.

However, teleconverters can degrade image quality. This can be particularly noticeable when shooting at maximum aperture. Results should improve when the lens is stopped down to f/8 or f/11; beyond this, sharpness may tail off again due to diffraction.

Converters also cause a loss of light. Fitting a 2x converter to an f/4 lens turns it

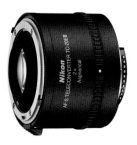

AF-S TELECONVERTER TC-20E III ⌃

into an effective f/8. The camera's autofocus may become sluggish or will only work with the central focus points.

> ### Tip
>
> *1.3x crop gives you an instant, weightless 1.3x teleconverter with no image degradation.*

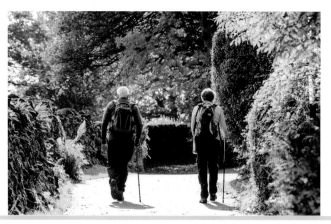

TRAVEL LIGHT «
Teleconverters are compact and easy to carry.
185mm, 1/250 sec., f/9, ISO 100.

ZOOMING IN »
Zoom lenses give you more framing options.
220mm, 1/500 sec., f/7.1, ISO 640.

» ZOOM LENSES

Zoom lenses have variable focal length, e.g. 18–105mm, as opposed to prime lenses, which have a single, fixed focal length, e.g. 35mm. A zoom lens can replace several prime lenses and cover the gaps in between, scoring highly for weight, convenience, and economy. Flexible focal length also allows very precise framing.

In terms of sharpness and image contrast, there is now little to choose between a good zoom and a good prime lens. Distortion can still be an issue. Most zoom lenses will have a "sweet spot", where distortion is minimal, somewhere in the zoom range, but still show discernible barrel distortion at wide settings and pincushion at the long end.

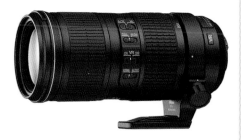

70-200MM F/4G ED AF-S VR NIKKOR ⌃

Cheaper zooms, and those with a very wide range (e.g. 18–200mm or 28–300mm) may still be optically compromised, and usually have a relatively small ("slow") maximum aperture, but prove useful for movie shooting in particular.

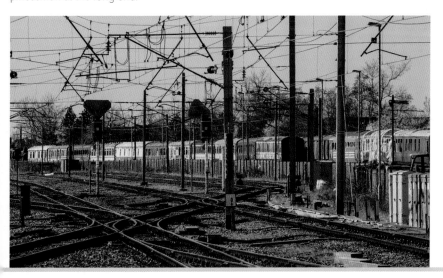

7 » PERSPECTIVE-CONTROL LENSES

Perspective-control (PC or "tilt and shift") lenses give unique flexibility in viewing and controlling the image. Their most obvious application is in photographing architecture, where, with a "normal" lens it often becomes necessary to tilt the camera upwards, resulting in converging verticals (buildings appear to lean back or even to one side). The shift function allows the camera back to be kept vertical, which in turn means that vertical lines in the subject remain vertical in the image. Tilt movements also allow extra control over depth of field—whether to extend or to minimize it.

The current Nikon range features three perspective-control lenses, with focal lengths of 24mm, 45mm, and 85mm. They retain many automatic functions, but require manual focusing.

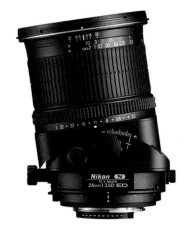

PC-E NIKKOR 24MM F/3.5D ED ⌃

CORRECTING DISTORTION ⌄
PC lenses help to eliminate leaning verticals (see original on left) in shots of tall subjects.
1/15 sec., f/11, ISO 200.

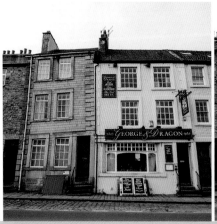
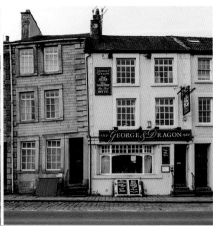

» NIKON LENS TECHNOLOGY

Many Nikkor lenses incorporate special features or materials, usually referred to by cryptic acronyms (as in the table below).

Brief explanations of the main terms are given here.

ABBREVIATION	TERM	EXPLANATION
AF	Autofocus	Lens focuses automatically. Most current Nikkor lenses are AF but manual focus lenses remain available.
CRC	Close-Range Correction	Advanced lens design that improves picture quality at close focusing distances.
D	Distance information	D-Type and G-Type lenses communicate information to the camera about the distance at which they are focusing, supporting functions like 3D Matrix Metering.
DC	Defocus-image Control	Found in a few specialized lenses; allows control of aberrations, altering how out-of-focus areas look.
DX	DX lens	Lenses specifically designed for DX-format digital cameras (see page 10).
G	G-Type lens	Modern Nikkor lenses with no aperture ring; aperture must be set by the camera.
ED	Extra-low Dispersion	ED glass minimizes chromatic aberration.
IF	Internal Focusing	Only internal elements of the lens move during focusing; the front element does not extend or rotate.
M/A	Manual/Auto	Many Nikkor AF lenses offer M/A mode, allowing seamless transition from automatic to manual focusing.
NC	Nano Crystal Coat	Said to virtually eliminate internal reflections within lenses, minimizing flare.
RF	Rear Focusing	Lens design where only the rearmost elements move during focusing—makes AF operation faster.
SWM	Silent Wave Motor	Special in-lens motors that deliver very fast and very quiet autofocus operation.
VR	Vibration Reduction	System that compensates for camera shake. VR is said to allow handheld shooting up to three stops slower than would otherwise be possible (for instance, 1/15th instead of 1/125 sec.). New lenses now feature VRII, said to gain an extra stop over VR (1/8th instead of 1/125 sec.).

Optical features/notes

DX lenses

Lens	
10.5mm f/2.8G Fisheye	CRC
10–24mm f/3.5–4.5G ED AF-S	ED, IF, SWM
12–24mm f/4G ED-IF AF-S	SWM
16–85mm f/3.5–5.6G ED VR AF-S	VRII, SWM
17–55mm f/2.8G ED-IF AF-S	ED, SWM
18–55mm f/3.5–5.6G VR II AF-S (Retractable)	VRII, SWM
18–55mm f/3.5–5.6G AF-S VR	VR, SWM
18–70mm f3.5–4.5G ED-IF AF-S	ED, SWM
18–105mm F/3.5–5.6G ED VR AF-S	ED, IF, VRII, NC, SWM
18–140mm F/3.5–5.6G ED VR AF-S	ED, IF, VRII, SWM
18–200mm f/3.5–5.6G ED AF-S VRII	ED, SWM, VRII
18–300mm f/3.5–5.6G ED VR AF-S	ED, IF, SWM, VRII
35mm f/1.8G AF-S	SWM
40mm f/2.8G AF-S Micro NIKKOR	SWM
55–200mm f/4–5.6G ED VR II	ED, SWM, VRII
55–200mm f/4–5.6 AF-S VR	ED, SWM, VR
55–300mm f/4.5–5.6G ED VR	ED, SWM
85mm f/3.5G ED VR AF-S Micro Nikkor	ED, IF, SWM, VRII

AF prime lenses

Lens	
14mm f/2.8D ED AF	ED, RF
16mm f/2.8D AF Fisheye	CRC

Angle of view on DX format (°)	Minimum focus distance (m)	Filter size	Dimensions (diameter/length, mm)	Weight (g)
180	0.14	Rear	63 x 62.5	300
109–61	0.24	77	82.5 x 87	460
99–61	0.3	77	82.5 x 90	485
83–18.5	0.38	67	72 x 85	485
79–28.5	0.36	77	85.5 x 11.5	755
76–28.5	0.28	52	66 x 59.5 (retracted)	195
76–28.5	0.28	52	73 x 79.5	265
76–22.5	0.38	67	73 x 75.5	420
76–15.3	0.45	67	76 x 89	420
76–11.5	0.45	67	78 x 97	490
76–8	0.5	72	77 x 96.5	560
76–5.3	0.45	77	83 x 120	830
44	0.3	52	70 x 52.5	210
38.5	0.163	52	68.5 x 64.5	235
28.5–8	1.1	52	70.5 x 83	300
28.5–8	1.1	52	73 x 99.5	335
28.5–5.2	1.4	58	76.5 x 123	530
18.5	0.28	52	73 x 98.5	355
90	0.2	Rear	87 x 86.5	670
120	0.25	Rear	63 x 57	290

Optical features/notes

20mm f/1.8G ED AF-S	ED, NC
20mm f/2.8D AF	CRC
24mm f/1.4G ED	ED, NC
24mm f/2.8D AF	
28mm f/1.8G AF-S	NC, SWM
28mm f/2.8D AF	
35mm f/2D AF	
35mm f/1.8G AF-S	RF, SWM
35mm f/1.4G AF-S	NC, SWM
50mm f/1.8G AF-S	SWM
50mm f/1.8D AF	
50mm f/1.4D AF	
50mm f/1.4G AF-S	IF, SWM
58mm f/1.4G AF-S	NC, SWM
85mm f/1.4G AF	SWM, NC
85mm f/1.8D AF	RF
85mm f/1.8G AF-S	IF, SWM
105mm f/2D AF DC	DC
135mm f/2D AF DC	DC
180mm f/2.8D ED-IF AF	ED, IF
200mm f/2G ED-IF AF-S VRII	ED, VRII, SWM
300mm f/4E PF ED VR AF-S	ED, SWM, NC, IF
300mm f/4D ED-IF AF-S	ED, IF
300mm f/2.8G ED VR II AF-S	ED, VRII, NC, SWM
400mm f/2.8G ED VR AF-S	ED, IF, VRII, NC
400mm f2.8E FL ED VR AF-S	ED, VR
400mm f/2.8D ED-IF AF-S II	ED, SWM

Angle of view on DX format (°)	Minimum focus distance (m)	Filter size	Dimensions (diameter/length, mm)	Weight (g)
70	0.2	77		355
70	0.25	62	69 x 42.5	270
61	0.25	77	83 x 88.5	620
61	0.3	52	64.5 x 46	270
53	0.25	67	73 x 80.5	330
53	0.25	52	65 x 44.5	205
44	0.25	52	64.5 x 43.5	205
44	0.25	58	72 x 71.5	305
44	0.3	67	83 x 89.5	600
31.3	0.45	58	72 x 52.5	185
31.3	0.45	52	63 x 39	160
31.3	0.45	52	64.5 x 42.5	230
31.3	0.45	58	73.5 x 54	280
27.3	0.58	72	85 x 70	385
18.5	0.85	77	86.5 x 84	595
18.5	0.85	62	71.5 x 58.5	380
18.5	0.8	67	80 x 73	350
15.2	0.9	72	79 x 111	640
12	1.1	72	79 x 120	815
9.1	1.5	72	78.5 x 144	760
8.2	1.9	52	124 x 203	2930
5.2	1.4	77	89 x 147.5	755
5.2	1.45	77	90 x 222.5	1440
5.2	2.2	52	124 x 267.5	2900
4	2.9	52	159.5 x 368	4620
4	2.6	40.5	159.5 x 358	3800
4	3.8	52	160 x 352	4800

Optical features/notes

500mm f/4G ED VR AF-S	IF, ED, VRII, NC
600mm f/4G ED VR AF-S	ED, IF, VRII, NC
800mm f/5.6E FL ED VR AF-S	ED, NC, SWM, FL
AF zoom lenses	
14–24mm f/2.8G ED AF-S	IF, ED, SWM, NC
16–35mm f/4G ED VR	NC, ED, VR
17–35mm f/2.8D ED-IF AF-S	IF, ED, SWM
18–35mm f/3.5–4.5G ED AF-S	ED, SWM
24–70mm f/2.8G ED AF-S	ED, SWM, NC
24–85mm f/2.8–4D IF AF	IF
24–85mm f/3.5–4.5G ED VR AF-S	ED, VRII, SWM
24–120mm f/4G ED-IF AF-S VR	ED, SWM, NC, VRII
28–300mm f/3.5–5.6G ED VR	ED, SWM
70–200mm f/2.8G ED-IF AF-S VRII	ED, SWM, VRII
70–200mm f/4G ED AF-S VRIII	ED, IF, SWM, NC, VRIII
70–300mm f/4.5–5.6G AF-S VR	ED, IF, SWM, VRII
80–400mm f/4.5–5.6D ED VR AF-S	ED, VR, NC
200–400mm f/4G ED-IF AF-S VRII	ED, NC,VRII, SWM
Macro lenses	
60mm f/2.8G ED AF-S Micro	ED, SWM, NC
105mm f/2.8G AF-S VR Micro	ED, IF, VRII, NC, SWM
200mm f/4D ED-IF AF Micro	ED, CRC
Perspective-control lenses	
24mm f/3.5D ED PC-E (manual focus)	ED, NC
45mm f/2.8D ED PC-E (manual focus)	ED, NC
85mm f/2.8D ED PC-E (manual focus)	ED, NC

Angle of view on DX format (°)	Minimum focus distance (m)	Filter size	Dimensions (diameter/length, mm)	Weight (g)
3.1	4	52	139.5 x 391	3880
2.4	5	52	166 x 445	5060
2	5.9	52	160 x 461	4590
90-61	0.28	None	98 x 131.5	970
83-44	0.29	77	82.5 x 125	680
79-44	0.28	77	82.5 x 106	745
76-44	0.28	77	83 x 95	385
61-22.50	0.38	77	83 x 133	900
61-18.5	0.5	72	78.5 x 82.5	545
61-18.5	0.38	72	78 x 82	465
61-13.5	0.45	77	84 x 103.5	710
53-5.2	0.5	77	83 x 114.5	800
22.5-8	1.4	77	87 x 209	1540
22.5-8	1	67	78 x 178.5	850
22.5-5.20		67	80 x 143.5	745
20-4	2.3	77	95.5 x 203	1570
8-4	2	52	124 x 365.5	3360
26.3	0.185	62	73 x 89	425
15	0.31	62	83 x 116	720
8	0.5	62	76 x 104.5	1190
56	0.21	77	82.5 x 108	730
34.5	0.25	77 x 94	83.5 x 112	780
18.9	0.39	77	82.7 x 107	650

ACCESSORIES AND CARE

Beyond lenses and flashguns, there are many other accessories which can extend the capabilities of the camera. Nikon's system is huge, and third-party suppliers offer even more options.

» ESSENTIALS

Nikon supplies several essential items with the camera. It's well worth considering the value of spares (notably spare batteries) and upgrades (e.g. for the strap). Small items like the body cap (BF-1A or BF-1B) and hotshoe cover (BS-1) are easily misplaced but cheap to replace.

› EN-EL15 battery

While the camera's battery life is good, it can't hurt to keep a fully charged spare on hand—especially in cold conditions, when using the monitor extensively, or when shooting movies. Third-party batteries are cheaper but may have a slightly lower power rating.

› Strap

The supplied strap is nice if you really feel the need to advertise that you're using a Nikon, but isn't particularly comfortable in extended use. There are many alternative straps and other carrying systems. I've recently been impressed by the Slide from Peak Design. It's also much easier to remove from the camera if you want to reduce clutter (e.g. for a long tripod session).

COASTING »

Long hikes to remote locations definitely make you think about what you carry and how you carry it. Forgetting anything essential can end in tears, but there can't be a serious outdoor photographer who has never found themselves without a spare battery or memory card or tripod attachment at some point in their career. *18mm, 1/200 sec., f/16, ISO 200.*

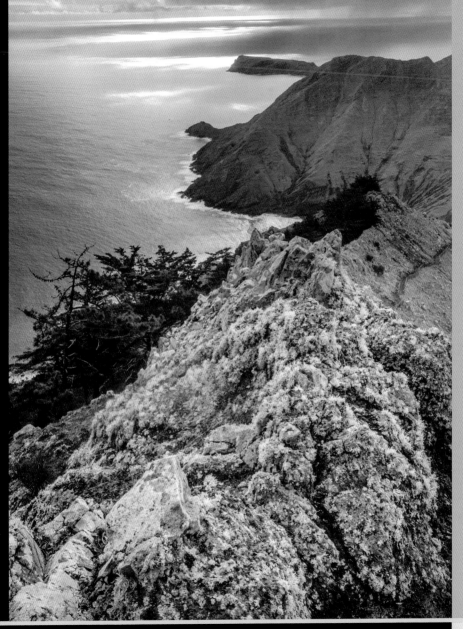

8 » FILTERS

Digital features, such as variable white balance, have made many filters virtually redundant. Effects like soft-focus and starburst, too, can be added in-camera via the Retouch menu. A far wider range of effects, with much greater finesse, is available in post-processing.

However, some filters still have value. A UV or skylight filter on each lens helps protect against damage, although many working pros rely purely on lens hoods.

› Polarizing filters

A polarizing filter reduces reflections, cutting glare and restoring transparency to water and glass. It can also cut through atmospheric haze and intensify colors in foliage and skies. The effect is strongest when shooting at right angles to the sunlight. It's almost impossible to replicate it in post-processing.

POLARIZER ⌄
A polarizing filter can intensify colors and accentuate clouds (as seen in the left side of this composite image).
50mm, 1/30 and 1/125 sec., f/11, ISO 100.

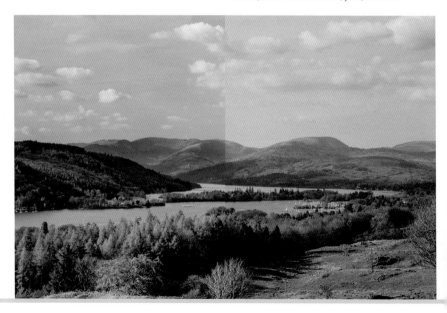

› Neutral-density filters

Neutral-density (ND) filters cut the amount of light reaching the lens. Plain ND filters let you set slower shutter speeds and/or wider apertures.

Graduated ND filters have been widely used in landscape photography to compensate for large differences in brightness between sky and land. However, the straight-line transition is often unpleasantly obvious against irregular skylines. The wide dynamic ranges of cameras like the D7200 greatly reduce the need for ND filters, especially when shooting RAW.

GRADUATED FILTER ❯❯
A graduated filter isn't much help here, and unpleasantly obvious too (inset). Shooting in RAW, with careful exposure and post-processing, I didn't need it anyway.
70mm, 1/80 sec., f/11, ISO 100, tripod.

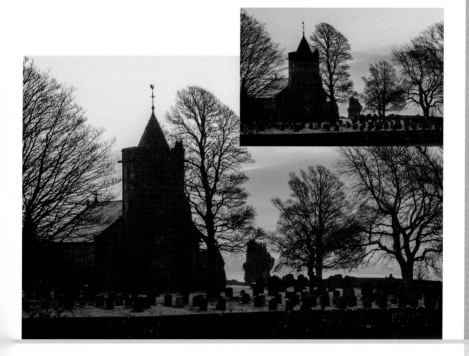

8 » OPTIONAL ACCESSORIES

Nikon is often criticized over the price of its accessories. Third-party alternatives are often far cheaper. However, take care to source reputable, fully compatible products.

› AC Adapter EH-5B and Power Connector EP-5A

This powers the camera directly from the AC mains, allowing uninterrupted shooting in long studio sessions or time-lapse sequences.

› Wireless Remote Control ML-L3

This inexpensive little unit lets you trigger the camera from up to 16ft (5m) away. There are receivers on both front and rear of the camera. Units like Hähnel's Giga T Pro II allow fuller control of the camera.

› GP-1 and GP-1A GPS units

Dedicated Global Positioning System devices (see page 230).

› ME-1 Stereo Microphone or ME-W1 Wireless Microphone

These microphones greatly improve sound quality in movie shooting.

› DK-20C viewfinder lenses

The viewfinder has built-in dioptric adjustment (page 24). For eyesight beyond its range, Nikon produces supplementary viewfinder lenses between −5 and +3 m^{-1}. However, for most people it's much easier to wear contact lenses or glasses.

› Screen shades

Camera LCD screens can be impossible to see properly in bright sunlight. The viewfinder is better for shooting in bright light, but you still need the screen for Live View, movie shooting, and image review. The best-known maker of screen shades is Hoodman.

» CAMERA SUPPORT

› Tripods

VR lenses, and the D7200's high ISO image quality, make handholding fully viable for many shots. Still, dynamic range is best at low ISO ratings, and some shots will always require solid support. Tripods are essential for serious movie shooting, too.

Titanium and carbon fiber combine low weight and good rigidity. They aren't cheap but a good tripod is an investment which should last for many years.

BEANBAG ⌄
A simple, homemade beanbag that has served me well for many years.

› Monopods

Monopods are light, easy to carry, and quick to set up. They are favored by sports photographers, who often need to react quickly while using hefty long telephoto lenses.

› Other camera support

There are many other proprietary products and improvised alternatives. It's hard to beat the humble beanbag, which can easily be homemade.

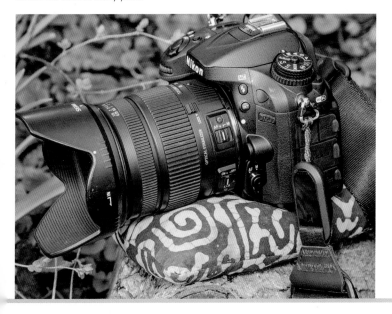

8 » CAMERA CASES

A case is arguably essential for outdoor use. A simple drop-in pouch, worn on a waist-belt, is most practical.

To carry a larger system, a backpack-type bag is kindest on your spine.

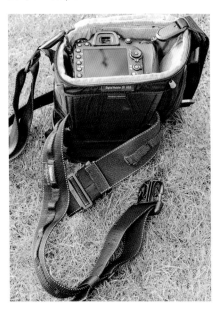

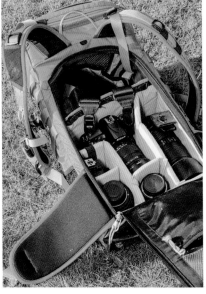

POUCH ⌃
A padded pouch (this one's by Think Tank Photo) combines good protection and easy access.

BACKPACK ⌃
Backpacks—this one's by f-stop—are best for the spine.

» STORING IMAGES

› Memory cards

The D7200 stores images on Secure Digital (SD), SDHC, and SDXC cards. On long trips it's easy to fill up even large-capacity memory cards. Prices have fallen, so it's advisable to carry a spare or two.

Memory card performance is measured in two ways: Speed rating (e.g. 30MB/s) and speed class rating (e.g. Class 10). Class 4 is adequate for most stills shooting but prolonged high-speed bursts or video shooting call for higher ratings.

› Backing up on the move

Memory cards rarely fail but it's always worth backing up valuable images as soon as possible. You can backup in-camera to Slot 2 (page 107). On longer trips without regular computer access, you can use a mobile device for further backup. Dedicated photo storage devices are becoming rare, supplanted by laptops, smartphones, or tablets.

› Card care

Blank cards are cheap but cards full of images are irreplaceable. SD cards are robust but it's still wise to treat them with care. Keep them in their original plastic cases, or something more substantial, and avoid exposure to extremes of temperature, liquids, and strong electromagnetic fields. (Modern airport X-ray machines aren't harmful to cameras or memory cards.)

SECURE STORAGE ⌄
A reasonably secure place to store spare or filled cards in the top of the backpack shown opposite.

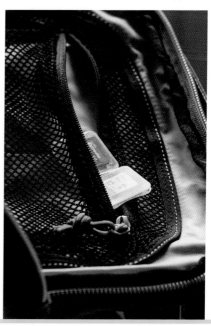

8 » CAMERA CARE

The D7200 is rugged, but it's also packed with complex and potentially delicate electronic and optical technology. A few simple precautions should help it keep functioning perfectly for many years.

› Basic care

Keeping the camera clean is fundamental. Keep it in a case when not in use. Remove dust and dirt with a blower, then wipe with a soft, dry cloth. Never touch the reflex mirror or shutter-blinds; both are extremely delicate. Remove dust from the mirror with gentle use of an air-blower, and nothing else.

If the rear screen needs cleaning, use a blower as above, then wipe the surface with a soft cloth or a swab designed for the purpose. Do not apply pressure and never use household cleaning fluids.

SAND, SEA, AND SPRAY ⌄
Shooting near the sea is potentially hazardous for cameras: salt spray is notoriously insidious. Sand, dust, and dirt all require care too.
200mm, 1/500 sec., f/10, ISO 200.

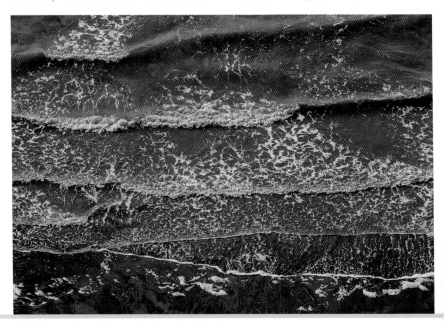

› Cleaning the sensor

Strictly speaking, it's not the sensor itself but its protective low-pass filter that concerns us. Dust on this will appear as spots in your images.

However careful you are, unless you never change lenses, some dust will eventually sneak in. Fortunately, the D7200 has a self-cleaning facility. You can activate it manually at any time, or set it to activate automatically when you switch the camera on and/or off (see Clean image sensor in the Setup menu, page 129).

Occasionally, stubborn spots may remain, making it necessary to clean the filter manually. Do this in a clean, draught-free, well-lit place. Ensure the battery is fully charged, or use a mains adapter. Remove the lens, switch the camera on and select **Lock mirror up for cleaning** from the Setup menu. Press the shutter-release button to lock up the mirror. First, attempt to remove dust using a hand-blower (**do not use** compressed air or any other aerosol). If this appears ineffective, consider using a dedicated cleaning swab, carefully following its instructions. **Do not** use other brushes or cloths and **never** touch the filter with your finger. When finished, turn the camera off and the mirror will reset.

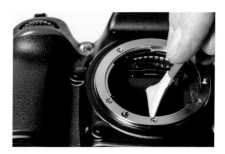

SENSOR CLEANING   ⌃
Cleaning the sensor requires great care.

Warning!

Any damage to the sensor from inappropriate manual cleaning could void your warranty. If in doubt, consult a dealer or professional camera repairer.

Tip

If (when!) spots do appear on the image, they can always be removed using, for example, the Clone tool or Healing brush in Adobe Photoshop. In Nikon Capture NX-D this process can be automated by creating a Dust-off reference image (page 129).

› Braving the elements

Cold

Nikon specify an operating temperature range of 32–104°F (0–40°C). When temperatures fall further, you can still use the camera, but aim to keep it within the specified range whenever possible. Keeping the camera in an insulated case or under your outer clothing between shots will help keep it warmer than the surroundings. If it does become chilled, battery life can be severely reduced (so carry a spare). In extreme cold, the displays may become erratic or disappear, and ultimately the camera may cease to function. If allowed to warm up gently, no permanent harm should result.

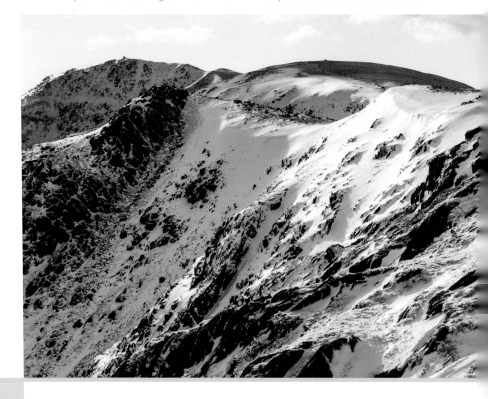

Heat and humidity

Extremes of heat and humidity (Nikon stipulate over 85%) can be even more problematic, and carry more risk of long-term damage. Rapid transfers from cool environments to hot and humid ones (air-conditioned hotel to sultry streets) can cause external and (more seriously) internal condensation. When anticipating such transitions, pack the camera and lens(es) in airtight containers with sachets of silica gel to absorb moisture. Allow equipment to reach ambient temperature before unpacking.

SNOW «
Living and working in the UK, I rarely encounter temperatures low enough to cause problems.
86mm, 1/800 sec., f/11, ISO 200.

CONDENSATION ⌄
Tempting as a warm café may be on a cold day, there's a risk of condensation on and even in a cold camera—best to pack it away whilst inside.
86mm, 1/60 sec., f/5.6, ISO 800.

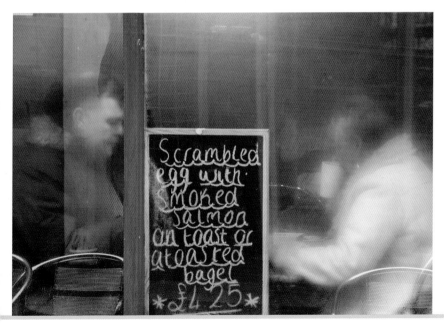

› Braving the elements

Water

The D7200 is reasonably weatherproof, so can be used with confidence in light rain. Still, keep exposure to a minimum, and wipe regularly with a microfiber cloth. Ensure all access covers on the camera are closed, avoid using the built-in flash, and keep the hotshoe cover in place. Take extra care around salt water. If contact does occur, clean carefully and immediately with a cloth lightly dampened with fresh water.

Ideally, protect the camera with a waterproof cover. A simple plastic bag will provide rudimentary protection, but purpose-made rain-guards give better protection and access to controls. Aquapac's reasonably priced DSLR case is a tight fit for the D7200, but can be used with a slimline lens.

SPLASH AND DASH
When in splash range, take care!
50mm, 1/500 sec., f/8, ISO 400.

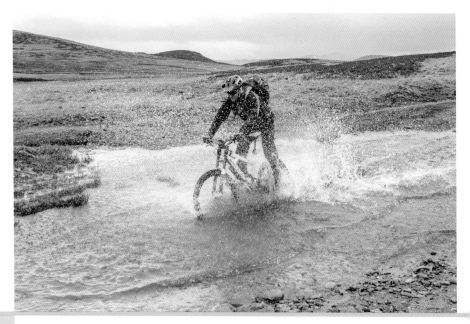

Dust

To minimize spots on images, and the need for sensor cleaning, try and avoid dust entering the camera. Above all, take care when changing lenses. Aim the camera downward and stand with your back to the wind. In really bad conditions (such as sandstorms) it's best not to change lenses at all. Preferably, protect the camera with a waterproof, and therefore dustproof, case. If dust settles on the outside of the camera, remove it carefully, using a hand-operated or compressed-air blower, before changing lenses, memory cards, or batteries. Keep all covers closed until the camera is clean.

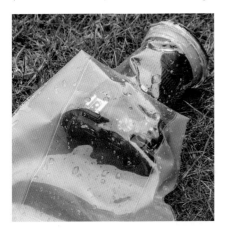

AN SLR CASE FROM AQUAPAC ⌃

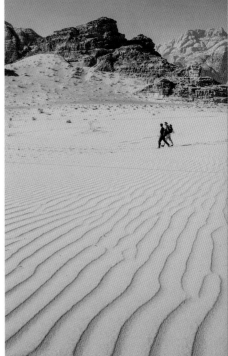

SANDY SHORES »
Sandy environments like deserts and beaches require great care when changing lenses.
18mm, 1/200 sec., f/11, ISO 100.

Connecting to external devices is integral to digital photography. In a way, taking the photograph is only the beginning—to make the most of your images, you need to store, organize, view, and print your images, and you will even need to take some time to process and edit them.

» CONNECTING TO A COMPUTER

Connecting to a Mac or PC allows you to store, organize, and backup your images. It also helps you exploit the full power of the D7200, including the ability to optimize image quality from RAW files.

A CD drive is no longer essential; there is no CD supplied with the camera and any software you may require is available to download. This makes it easier to consider alternatives to Nikon's own apps for handling your images and video.

› Computer requirements

The large file sizes produced by the D7200 are demanding on processor speed, hard disk capacity, and memory (RAM), for which 4GB is a suggested minimum. Fortunately, adding extra RAM is (usually) easy and inexpensive. Extra hard disk space can also be helpful, as the system will slow significantly when the hard disk becomes close to capacity. Photos gobble up hard drive space and videos even more so.

The D7200 supports USB3 for connecting the camera, and a suitable cable is supplied. USB3 is compatible with USB2 but transfer speeds over USB2 will be slower. You can also use a card-reader (see page 222).

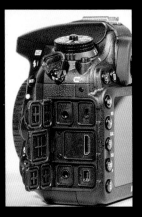

**CONNECTION PORTS
ON THE LEFT SIDE
OF THE D7200**

A D7200 CONNECTED TO A COMPUTER »

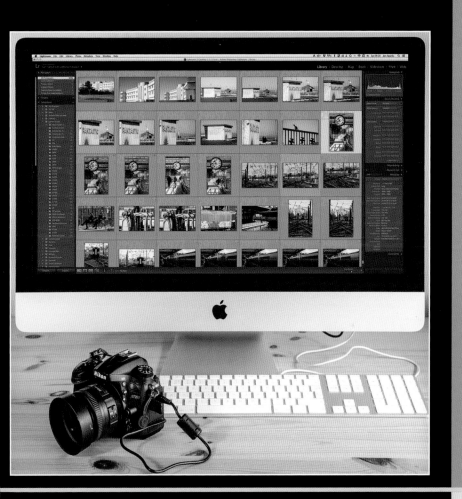

9

› Importing photos

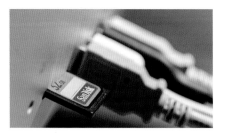

**BUILT-IN SD CARD SLOT
ON A MODERN IMAC** ⌃

Onboard Wi-Fi doesn't let you transfer images to a laptop or desktop. This normally requires a physical connection, using the supplied USB cable or a card-reader. The latter is usually easier. Many modern computers have built-in SD card slots.

The exact procedure depends on the software you are using. Nikon Transfer, supplied with View NX-i, is simple to use and facilitates backup of photos during import. However, if you're using an app like iPhoto or Lightroom (strongly recommended—see below) to manage your photos, it's best to use this for import too.

Whatever software you use, there are several issues to consider, including whether to backup automatically on import. You also need to decide where on your hard drive(s) photos should be stored. You may also wish to rename files, and perhaps apply keywords, as they are imported.

It's usually best to import movies separately. You will probably want to store them in a different folder to still images. Often it's better to import movies through your movie editing software.

**IMPORT OPTIONS IN
ADOBE LIGHTROOM** ⌄

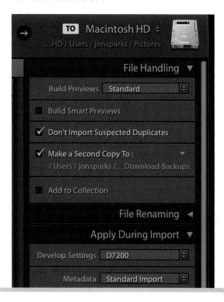

› Backing up

Initially, each image exists only as data on the camera's memory card (both cards, if you use Slot 2 for **Backup**—see page 107). When you transfer images to the computer and format the card(s) for reuse, images again exist in just one location, the computer's hard drive. Any mishap or failure of that hard drive could erase thousands of irreplaceable images.

You can backup photos during import, but this means backing up duplicates, rejects, and other duds too. You may prefer to backup after an initial weeding process—but don't leave it too long. The simplest form of backup is to a second hard drive; the "gold standard" requires multiple drives, one always kept off-site. Online backup is another option. Flickr offers an impressive 1TB, completely free, but does not support RAW files. Paid, but relatively affordable, services like Google Drive and Dropbox Pro give greater flexibility and security.

APPLE'S TIME MACHINE MAINTAINS ⌄⌄
BACKUPS AUTOMATICALLY

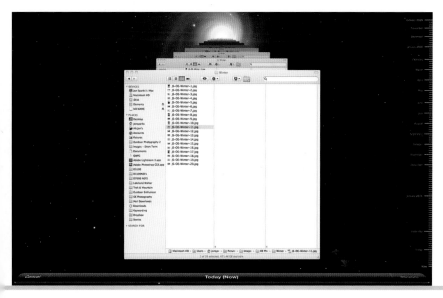

> ## Color calibration

> ## Wi-Fi

It's a common headache: images look one way on the camera back, different on your computer screen, different on a friend's screen, and different again when printed. Achieving real consistency across different devices requires color management. This is a complex subject and detailed advice is beyond the scope of this book; there's more in the *Digital SLR Handbook* (from this author and publisher) and a good summary at *www.cambridgeincolour.com/tutorials/color-management1.htm*.

Above all, it's vital that your main computer screen is calibrated. This might appear time-consuming but ultimately saves much time and frustration.

The D7200 has onboard Wi-Fi. While this is welcome, its capabilities are rather limited. It will only connect to mobile devices (iOS or Android), not laptop or desktop computers. Wirelessly transferring images to a computer is easy (if slow) with an Eye-Fi card (see page 226) but it's irritating that onboard Wi-Fi doesn't support it.

Further, Nikon's claim that you can "control the camera remotely" is wildly overstated; you can set focus and trigger the shutter, but that's all. Finally, it doesn't work with movies.

Still, Nikon's Wireless Mobile Utility is free, simple to set up (especially on iOS devices), and easy to use. For Android

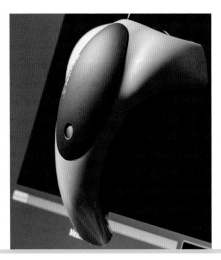

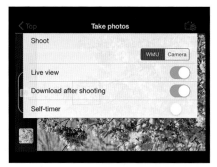

TAKING PHOTOS WITH NIKON WIRELESS MOBILE UTILITY ⌃

CALIBRATION IN PROGRESS WITH DATACOLOR SPYDER4EXPRESS ⌃

devices which support NFC (Near Field Communication), connection is simply a matter of touching the device's antenna to the 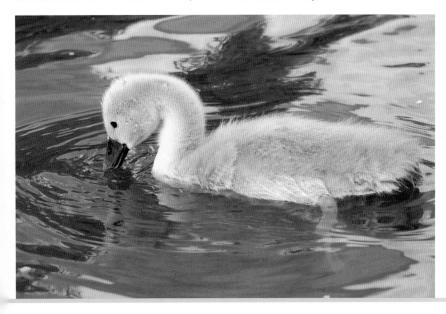 logo on the camera.

The app lets you view and transfer photos already on the camera, and take new shots. However, because you can't change camera settings within the app, you need to get all settings, including Live View focusing options sorted beforehand.

In Wide-area AF or Normal area AF, you can focus by tapping the subject on the device screen. You can't zoom in (as you can on the camera) for a precise focus check. However, the preview on an iPad or other tablet is significantly larger than the camera's screen.

WATCH THE BIRDIE!   ⌄
Remote shooting minimizes disturbance to shy subjects.
450mm, 1/500 sec., f/4, ISO 400.

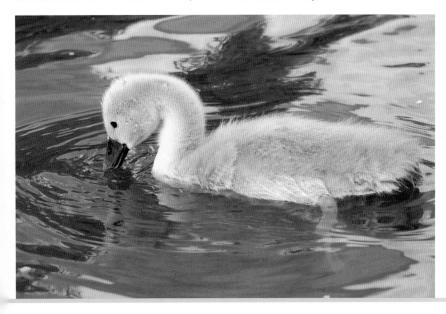

› Eye-Fi

Eye-Fi looks like a regular SD card, but includes a Wi-Fi antenna, allowing you to transfer images wirelessly. Some Eye-Fi cards also support ad-hoc networks, allowing images to be transferred to a laptop or iPad anywhere. However, transfer speeds are slow. This is particularly noticeable when shooting RAW.

EYE-FI ⩔
Eye-Fi's latest mobiPRO card has 32Gb of storage as well as Wi-Fi.

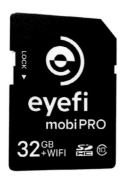

› Tethered shooting

Tethered shooting allows you to operate the D7200 from an external device, and to transfer images directly. Nikon's Wireless Mobile Utility is a very rudimentary example. Other apps, like Nikon Camera Control Pro 2 (optional purchase), go much further. It allows full control of the camera from a Mac or PC, integrating Live View for real-time viewing. However it requires either a physical (USB) connection or a very expensive network adapter kit (Nikon UT-1WK): you can't use onboard Wi-Fi. Lightroom and several other apps also support tethered shooting via USB.

For wireless shooting, a more affordable solution is the CamRanger, which supports Live View and gives control of all main camera settings. It can link to iOS and Android devices, Macs, and PCs. It requires a short USB link to the camera but can connect wirelessly to the controlling device over a range of around 164ft (50m). It creates its own network so can be used anywhere.

› Software and image processing

There are many things we may do with our images after shooting—organizing, backing up, printing, sharing, and making them look their best. All require the right software.

Software choice depends partly on how you shoot. If you always shoot JPEG images, you may feel little need to tinker with them later, so organizing and cataloging will be your main priorities. If you shoot RAW files, on the other hand, post-processing is essential—and gives you great freedom to adjust tone, color, and many other attributes to your liking.

Nikon software

The D7200 is one of the first Nikon DSLRs not to be supplied with a software CD. However, Nikon View NX-i software, which has recently replaced Nikon View NX2, is available as a free download from the Nikon web site. The package includes the aforementioned Nikon Transfer.

Unlike View NX2, View NX-i (see below) is purely a browser and organizer. Its organizing/cataloging functions have certainly been beefed up compared to its

NIKON VIEW NX-i

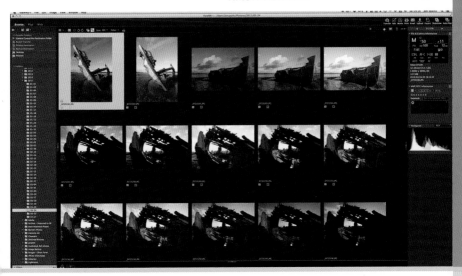

predecessor, but none of it seems particularly fast or intuitive. What's more, as soon as you need to perform even the most basic image-editing/enhancement operations, images must be opened in Nikon Capture NX-D.

Nikon Capture NX-D

Nikon Capture NX-D has recently supplanted Capture NX2. Some changes are welcome, including the price (it's free). Editing is now non-destructive, and batch processing has been improved, so it should be faster and more intuitive. However, many advanced tools have been removed. The separation of organizing/cataloging (View NX-i) and image-editing (Capture NX-D) does remove much of the overlap which previously existed between the two

programs. However, when you are used to the seamless integration of these two key processes in apps like Lightroom, Nikon's approach seems like a step backward.

Third-party software

The undisputed market leader is Adobe Photoshop. Adobe has recently changed to a subscription model under the Creative Cloud label, which means that the software is continuously updated—but it will stop working if you don't keep up the subscription payments.

Photoshop's feature set is vast, and many users' needs are amply covered by the more affordable Photoshop Elements. It has sophisticated editing features

ADOBE PHOTOSHOP CC

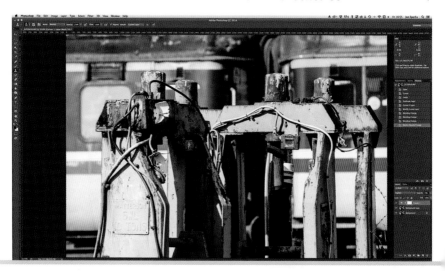

including the ability to open RAW files. Its Organizer module lets you "tag" photos, assign them to "Albums", or add keywords. Elements is not part of Creative Cloud: you pay once for a perpetual licence to use the software, in the familiar way.

Many Mac users have been happy with the free iPhoto, which also unifies organizing and editing. However, Apple has announced that iPhoto (and Aperture) are being discontinued in favor of a single Photos app. This has most of the functionality of iPhoto but few of Aperture's advanced features.

Complete integration of organizing and editing was pioneered by Aperture (Mac only) and Adobe Lightroom (Mac and PC). The imminent demise of Aperture leaves Lightroom in a near-monopoly position, though Corel's AfterShot Pro may challenge this.

Highly recommended, especially if you shoot RAW, Lightroom offers powerful organizing/cataloging, integrated with advanced image editing for seamless workflow. Editing is "non-destructive": all your edit settings such as color balance, exposure, and cropping are recorded alongside the original RAW file. TIFF or JPEG versions, incorporating your edits, can be exported when needed. A Creative Cloud Photography subscription includes both Photoshop and Lightroom, or you can buy Lightroom or Photoshop Elements as a one-off purchase.

ADOBE LIGHTROOM'S DEVELOP MODULE ⌄ OFFERS A VERY WIDE SPECTRUM OF RAW ADJUSTMENTS

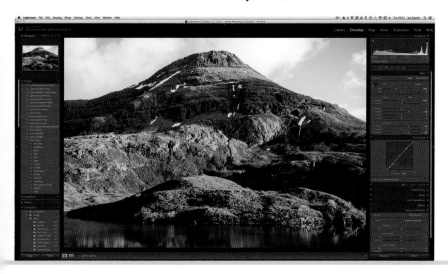

9 » GPS

Nikon's GP-1 or GP-1a GPS (Global Positioning System) units mount in the hotshoe or clip to the camera strap. They link to the camera's accessory terminal using a supplied cable. Certain third-party GPS units can also be attached.

GPS units add information on location, altitude, heading, and time to each image's metadata. This can be viewed as an extra info page during playback (page 96) and can be read by many imaging apps.

When the camera is connected and receiving data from the GPS, **GPS** shows in the information display. If this flashes, the GPS is searching for a signal, and no data is recorded.

Set GPS options via **Location data** in the Setup menu.

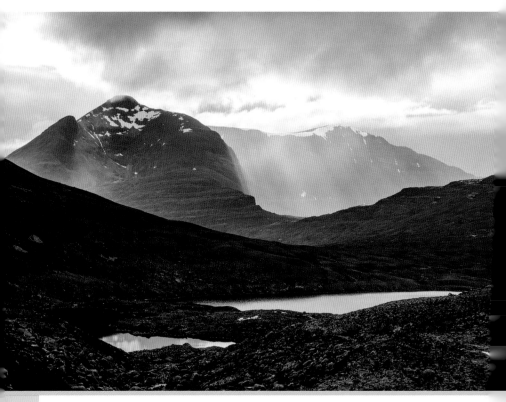

› Standby timer

Disable stops the meters turning off and returning the camera to standby. This should ensure a stable connection to the GPS satellites. If you select **Enable**, the meters will turn off after 1 minute, saving battery power. However, next time you take a picture, the GPS receiver may not have time to get a fix, in which case no location data will be recorded.

› Position

Displays the current information as reported by the GPS device.

› Set clock from satellite

The GPS network embodies extremely accurate timing. Setting **Enable** should keep your camera clock bang on.

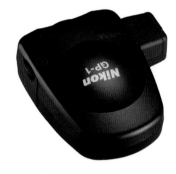

NIKON GP-1 GPS CLIPS INTO THE HOTSHOE ☆

LOCATION, LOCATION ‹‹
GPS is perfect for recording exactly where shots were taken, but keep an eye on battery life.
65mm, 1/400 sec., f/8, ISO 200.

9 » CONNECTING TO A PRINTER

For maximum flexibility and control when printing, transfer photographs to a computer first. The procedure then depends on your operating system, imaging software, and the printer you are using. It's now also easy to print from iOS or Android devices.

Occasionally you may still wish to print directly from the camera or memory card. The card can be inserted into a compatible printer or taken to a photo printing store. Alternatively, the camera can be connected to any printer that supports PictBridge. Only JPEG files can be printed in this way. To print from RAW files, create JPEG copies first (page 138).

When you connect directly to a printer using the supplied USB cable and turn the camera on, the camera back displays a welcome screen, followed by a PictBridge playback display.

To print the displayed picture, simply press (OK). This reveals a menu of printing options, including **Page size**, **No of copies** (1–99), **Border**, **Time stamp**, and **Crop**. Setting Crop options is similar to using **Trim** in the Retouch menu (page 135). Having set options, select **Start printing** and press (OK).

For other options, press **MENU**. **Print select** allows you to select one or more images. Hold 🔍 and use ▲/▼ to set the number of copies for each. You can also create an **Index Print** of all JPEG images (up to a maximum of 256) on the memory card. **Select date** prints one copy of each picture taken on selected date(s). **Print (DPOF)** prints images already selected using **Print set (DPOF)** in the Playback menu (page 104).

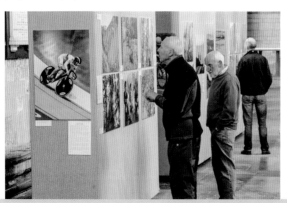

TV SHOW »
A TV can replace the old-fashioned slide-projector and screen as a way of showing images to family and friends.
200mm, 1/500 sec., f/14, ISO 400.

GALLERY «
Exhibition images will require careful work on the computer before professional printing.

» CONNECTING TO A TV

You can play photos and movie clips through an HDMI TV or set-top box.

1) Check settings via **HDMI** in the Setup menu.

2) Turn the camera off (**always do this before connecting or disconnecting the cable**).

3) Open the HDMI cover on the left side of the camera and insert the cable into the slot. Connect the other end to the TV.

4) Tune the TV to an HDMI channel.

5) Turn the camera on and press ▶. Images remain visible on the camera monitor as well as on the TV and you navigate using the multi-selector in the usual way. You can use Slide show (Playback menu, page 104) to automate playback.

> **Note:**
> A mains adapter is recommended for lengthy playback sessions. No harm should result if the camera's battery expires during playback, but it is annoying.

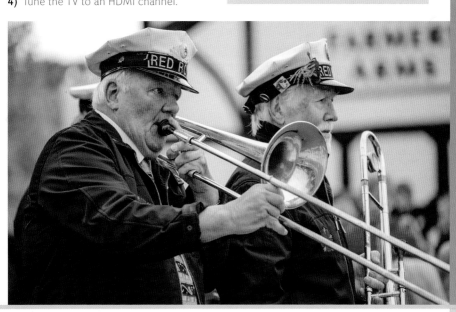

» GLOSSARY

8-bit, 14-bit, 16-bit *See Bit depth.*

Aperture The adjustable lens opening which admits light. Relative aperture sizes are expressed in f-numbers (see below).

Artifact Occurs when data or data produced by the sensor is interpreted incorrectly, resulting in visible flaws in the image.

Bit depth The amount of information recorded for each color channel. 8-bit, for example, means that the data distinguishes 2^8 or 256 levels of brightness for each channel. 16-bit images recognize over 65,000 levels per channel, which allows greater freedom in editing. The D7200 records RAW images in 12- or 14-bit depth and they are converted to 16-bit on import to the computer.

Bracketing Taking a number of otherwise identical shots in which just one parameter (e.g. exposure) is varied.

Buffer On-board memory that holds images until they can be written to the memory card.

Burst A number of frames shot in quick succession; the maximum burst size is limited by buffer capacity.

Channel The D7200, like other digital devices, records data for three separate color channels (*see RGB*).

Chimping Checking images on the screen after shooting.

Clipping Complete loss of detail in highlight or shadow areas of the image (sometimes both), leaving them as blank white or black.

CMOS (Complementary Metal Oxide Semiconductor) A type of image sensor used in many digital cameras, including the D7200.

Color temperature The color of light, expressed in degrees Kelvin (K). Confusingly, "cool" (blue) light has a higher color temperature than "warm" (red) light.

CPU (Central Processing Unit) A small computer in the camera (also found in many lenses) that controls most or all of the unit's functions.

Crop factor *See Focal length multiplication factor.*

Diopter Unit expressing the power of a lens.

dpi (dots per inch) A measure of resolution—should strictly be applied only to printers (*see ppi*).

Dynamic range The range of brightness from shadows to highlights within which the camera can record detail.

Exposure Used in several senses. For instance, "an exposure" is virtually synonymous with "an image" or "a photo": to make an exposure = to take a picture. Exposure also refers to the amount of light hitting the image sensor, and to systems of measuring this. *See also Overexposure, Underexposure.*

EV (Exposure Value) A standardized unit of exposure. 1 Ev halves or doubles the amount of light and is equivalent to 1 "stop" in traditional photographic parlance.

Extension rings/extension tubes Hollow tubes which fit between the camera tube and lens, used to allow greater magnifications.

f-number Lens aperture expressed as a fraction of focal length; f/2 is a wide aperture and f/16 is narrow.

Fast (lens) Lens with a wide maximum aperture, e.g. f1.8; f/4 is relatively fast for long telephotos.

Fill-in flash Flash used in combination with daylight. Used with naturally backlit or harshly side-lit subjects to prevent dark shadows.

Filter A piece of glass or plastic placed in front of, within, or behind the lens to modify light.

Firmware Software which controls the camera. Upgrades are issued by Nikon from time to time and can be transfered to the camera via a memory card.

Focal length The distance (in mm) from the optical center of a lens to the point at which light is focused.

Focal length multiplication factor Because the D7200's sensor is smaller than a frame of 35mm film, the effective focal length of all lenses is multiplied by 1.5.

fps (frames per second) The number of exposures (photographs) that can be taken in a second. The D7200's maximum rate is 5fps.

Gamut The range of colors and tones which can be captured in a digital file.

Highlights The brightest areas of the scene and/or the image.

Histogram A graph representing the distribution of tones in an image, ranging from pure black to pure white.

ISO (International Standards Organisation) ISO ratings express film speed and the sensitivity of digital sensors is quoted as ISO-equivalent.

JPEG (from Joint Photographic Experts Group) A compressed image file standard. High levels of JPEG compression can reduce files to about 5% of their original size, but not without some loss of quality.

LCD (Liquid Crystal Display) Flat screen, such as the D7200's rear monitor.

Macro A term used to describe close focusing and close-focusing ability of a lens. A true macro lens has a reproduction ratio of 1:1 or better.

Megapixel *See Pixel*.

Memory card A removable storage device for digital cameras.

Noise Image interference manifested as random variations in pixel brightness and/or color.

Overexposure When too much light reaches the sensor, resulting in a too-bright image, often with clipped highlights.

Pixel (picture element) The individual colored dots (usually square) which make up a digital image. One million pixels = 1 megapixel.

Post-processing Adjustment to images on computer after shooting. Can cover anything from minor tweaks of brightness or color to extensive editing.

Prime lens Lens with a single fixed focal length, e.g. 50mm.

ppi (pixels per inch) Should be applied to digital files rather than the commonly used dpi.

Reproduction ratio The ratio between the real size of an object and the size of its image on the sensor.

Resolution The number of pixels for a given dimension, for example, 300 pixels per inch. Resolution is often confused with *image size*. The native size of an image from the D7200 is 6000 x 4000 pixels; this could make a large but coarse print at 100 dpi or a smaller but finer one at 300 dpi.

RGB (red, green, blue) Digital devices, including the D7200, record color in terms of brightness levels of the three primary colors.

Sensor The light-sensitive chip at the heart of every digital camera.

Shutter The mechanism which controls the amount of light reaching the sensor by opening and closing to expose the sensor when the shutter-release button is pressed.

Speedlight Nikon's range of dedicated external flashguns.

Spot metering A metering system which takes its reading from the light reflected by a small portion of the scene.

Telephoto lens A lens with a long focal length and a narrow angle of view.

TIFF (Tagged Image File Format) A universal file format supported by virtually all image-editing applications.

TTL (through the lens) The viewing and metering of SLR cameras such as the D7200.

Underexposure When insufficient light reaches the sensor, resulting in a too-dark image, often with clipped shadows.

USB (Universal Serial Bus) A data transfer standard, used to connect to a computer.

Viewfinder An optical system used for framing the image. On an SLR camera, such as the D7200, it shows the view as seen through the lens.

White balance A function which compensates for different color temperatures so that images may be recorded with correct color balance.

Wideangle lens A lens with a short focal length and a wide angle of view.

Zoom A lens with variable focal length, giving a range of viewing angles. To zoom in is to change focal length to give a narrower view and zoom out is the converse. Optical zoom refers to the genuine zoom ability of a lens; digital zoom is the cropping of part of an image.

» USEFUL WEB SITES

NIKON-RELATED SITES

Nikon Worldwide
Home page for the Nikon Corporation
www.nikon.com

Nikon UK
Home page for Nikon UK
www.nikon.co.uk

Nikon USA
Home page for Nikon USA
www.nikonusa.com

Nikon User Support
European Technical Support Gateway
www.europe-nikon.com

Nikon Historical Society
Worldwide site for study of Nikon products
www.nikonhs.org

Grays of Westminster
Revered Nikon-only London dealer
www.graysofwestminster.co.uk

GENERAL SITES

Digital Photography Review
Independent news and reviews
www.dpreview.com

Thom Hogan
Real-world reviews and advice
www.bythom.com/nikon.htm

Jon Sparks
Landscape and outdoor pursuits photography
www.jon-sparks.co.uk

EQUIPMENT

Adobe
Photoshop, Photoshop Elements, Lightroom
www.adobe.com/uk

Aquapac
Waterproof cases
www.aquapac.net

CamRanger
Remote camera control
http://camranger.com

f-stop
Backpacks and accessories
http://fstopgear.com

Peak Design
Camera carrying solutions
https://peakdesign.com

Sigma
Independent lenses and flash units
www.sigma-imaging-uk.com

PHOTOGRAPHY PUBLICATIONS

Photography books
Ammonite Press
www.ammonitepress.com

***Black & White Photography* magazine,
Outdoor Photography magazine**
www.thegmcgroup.com

» INDEX